AUM SHINRIKYO AND JAPANESE YOUTH

Daniel A. Metraux

University Press of America, Inc.
Lanham · New York · Oxford

Copyright © 1999 by
University Press of America,® Inc.
4720 Boston Way
Lanham, Maryland 20706

12 Hid's Copse Rd.
Cumnor Hill, Oxford OX2 9JJ

Library of Congress Cataloging-in-Publication Data

Metraux, Daniel Alfred.
Aum Shinrikyo and Japanese youth / Daniel A. Metraux.
p.   cm.
Includes bibliographical references and index.
1. Oumu Shinrikyō (Religious organization) 2. Youth—
Japan—Religious life. I. Title.
BP605.088M48 1999 299'.93—dc21   99—27942 CIP

ISBN 0-7618-1417-5 (pbk: alk. ppr.)

Contents

Preface

The terrorist sarin gas attack that killed 12 Tokyo subway commuters and injured nearly 6,000 more during the morning rush hour of March 20, 1995 shocked the world. Police immediately focused their investigation on Aum Shinrikyo[1], a small but already well-known religious sect[2] founded by Asahara Shoko in 1984. Asahara had gained notoriety for his prophecies that the destruction of contemporary society would occur shortly through a cataclysmic world war, Armageddon. Further investigation revealed that Aum[3] and its top leaders were guilty not only of two large-scale terrorist attacks, but also kidnapping, the murder of over two dozen innocent Japanese, drugging and the production of illegal drugs, the production of weapons of mass murder including poisonous gas, and conspiracy to commit armed insurrection. Although relatively new and small by Japanese standards, the sect had achieved public notoriety through its campaigns for public support, including a widely covered political campaign to elect its leaders to the Japanese Diet in 1990. Aum's posture as a world-rejecting movement that sought to build communes ("Lotus Villages") across Japan and its 1992 religious crusade in Russia also brought substantial public attention.

Aum Shinrikyo claimed over 10,000 members in the spring of 1995, including 1,100 "renunciates" (*shukke*), members who followed Aum's world-renouncing lifestyle. A membership list discovered by police in 1995 indicates that Aum's members were young—47.5% of the *shukke* were in their 20s and that 75.4 percent were in their 20s and 30s. Aum, however, was not entirely a youth movement. It had a proportionate share of middle-aged and elderly members, especially in its early days.

Scholars of Japanese religion have already published noteworthy works on Aum's history, theology, and leadership.[4] While Asahara and his immediate braintrust have received considerable attention, scholars have paid comparatively less attention to Aum's ordinary members—those who joined the sect for religious and social reasons and were generally uninvolved

v

in their leaders' terroristic and criminal activities. The primary goal of this work is to explore several questions about those ordinary members: Why did they join? What were their goals and expectations? Why did they choose to stay in or quit the sect?

A secondary goal of this work is to examine how the Aum phenomenon reflects a growing sense of alienation among some younger and middle-aged Japanese and why some of them are turning to religious groups such as Aum for answers. Tokyo University scholar and professor Shimazono Susumu writes that "Young people throughout the world are looking for something to replace modern concepts of freedom and rationality, and have begun to place their hopes in religious precepts, ascetic morality, meditation, and experiences of the mysterious." Shimazono asserts that the trend away from secularism back to religion, which began in the mid-1970s among the youth of many cultures worldwide, is caused at least in part by "The worsening of the environmental situation and of the problems accompanying urbanization (such as increased crime, poverty, and family breakdown...)" These problems have "engendered doubts concerning rationalism, science, and the ability of the secular state to further the welfare of its citizens....The development of Aum Shinrikyo's universe of belief is not unrelated to this worldwide return to religion by the young."[5]

At its start Aum was not the criminal monster the world discovered in 1995. Aum commenced as a benign religious group with traits common to other Japanese new religions: the presence of an idolized charismatic leader, a syncretic doctrine, and communal living. These features plus Asahara's stance as a strong anti-establishment figure made Aum attractive to thousands of mainly young Japanese.

I wish to acknowledge the hospitality and generosity of The International Exchange Office of Doshisha Women's College and its Director, Professor Takemura Kenichi[6], who provided me with a sumptuous apartment, office space and clerical help, and use of his college's fine library for my research over a five-month period. His staff, Kuroda Yoshihiro and Takeuchi Akihiro, also provided considerable assistance. Professors Morita Akira, Bernard Susser and other Doshisha Women's College faculty provided time and help. The research staff and faculty at the Nanzan Institute for Religion and Culture generously provided office space, room and board, and use of their excellent library. I am most grateful to Professors James Heisig, Paul Swanson, and Robert Kisala for their hospitality and considerable assistance.

This research was greatly assisted by a Travel Grant from the Association for Asian Studies.

I am grateful for the scholarly assistance of Professors Ian Reader, Sterling University, and Robert Grotjohn, Mary Baldwin College, and Ben Dorman, a doctoral candidate at Australia National University, and Andy Sumimoto of Soka Gakkai International for their critical reading of the first draft of this manuscript. Various officials at the Soka Gakkai including Hiromu Yamaguchi and Nishiguchi Hiroshi provided interesting perspectives on the Aum Affair. My former student and Research Assistant, Watanabe Yuki, provided some useful articles, reflections and translations. Jen Ragan Dorough and Tarah Blazek, students at Mary Baldwin College, provided invaluable clerical help. James Lott, Dean of Mary Baldwin College, provided valuable encouragement, generous funding, and extra time to work on this manuscript.

I must not forget Veronica Vicente, Anne-Louise Lasley, Elizabeth Lawson Nelson, and Clive Pemberton. Wilton and Virginia Dillon, Lewis and Nancy Hill, Dorothy Ling, and Linda Lussier. Their kindness and devotion have added new meaning to my life. Finally and most importantly, I wish to thank my beloved wife Judy for her loving support and willingness to live alone for many months while I pursued this research, my daughter, Katie, and my son, David, for their love. I wish to dedicate this work to my son, David Russell Metraux, a highly successful student at Syracuse University, who hopefully someday soon will return to Japan to discover the wonders of this country on his own.

Daniel A. Metraux
Nanzan Institute for Religion and Culture
Nagoya, Japan

Summer 1998

Chapter I

ଽ୭ଔ

Aum Shinrikyo and the Aum Generation

A um Shinrikyo's horrific sarin gas attack on thousands of unsuspecting subway commuters on 20 March 1995 raised a plethora of questions concerning Japanese society. A common query was why several thousand Japanese, many of them young and well-educated, would join a religious organization which ultimately killed over two dozen innocent victims and destroyed the lives of so many others.

Although each devotee had a highly personal reason for joining Aum, many of them had difficulty finding a role for themselves in mainstream Japanese society. They could not adopt society's values and life style and reacted strongly against the materialism of "bubble-economy" Japan. Unlike various other modern societies, Japan has no real safe haven for those of its citizens who abstain from orthodox values. "There is no effective, normal, subsocial system that can absorb people who cannot function in mainstream society."[1] Every generation of young Japanese contains numerous men and women who are discontented with one or more aspects of contemporary life, and each seeks outlets for this frustration. The middle-aged generation that now governs Japan produced political activists in the 1960s who shut down Tokyo University and other institutions of higher learning, demonstrated against the Japan-U.S. Security Treaty, and called for further democratization of Japanese society. Indeed, the student movement of a generation ago served as an important outlet for youthful discontent.

Many younger Japanese in the 1990s, however, feel alienated from politics. There is also a growing supposition that political action is itself useless. Some of the more unconventional younger Japanese of the 1990s sought solace in the spiritual world. A few even joined new *avant-garde* religious organizations such as Agonshu and Aum Shinrikyo. Asahara Shoko, the founder and leader of Aum Shinrikyo, emerged during the early 1990s as an often-interviewed anti-establishment figure who convinced many younger Japanese that he had the solutions for the problems affecting their lives and that Aum Shinrikyo was at the forefront of a new society in which life indeed would be much better.

Some scholars quite correctly question the use of Aum itself as a model for a discussion of alienation and religiosity in Japanese society. Ian Reader notes, for example:

> One critical element in Aum's alienation from society was because of its rejection by the vast majority of people. Asahara saw himself in competition with Kofuku and Agonshu [two rival sects]—and yet his movement barely recruited followers in years when Kofuku and Agonshu were increasing their numbers by many thousands. Aum's failure—and the repeated conflicts it ran into—were because the Japanese people as a whole and the young people it targeted, did not get taken in by it. So what is to stop someone from arguing that Aum demonstrated the strengths of the Japanese system, especially the religious system? If Japanese society is so rotten, and its young so incapable of comprehending the nature of religious leaders, why didn't Aum succeed in its recruitment drives?[2]

Reader's point is well-taken. However, Aum did attract more than 10,000 mainly young members and the interest of thousands more. Some Japanese journalists and scholars have gone so far as to call today's young Japanese the "Aum generation." This expression is certainly a gross exaggeration— the vast majority of young Japanese today regard themselves as part of mainstream society and plan "normal" carriers and lives. Many others, however, do not want to replicate the careers of their parents; they are not satisfied with the futures that society expects from them. Many do have legitimate religious concerns. Some are seeking an alternative way of life.

New Religions scholar Robert Kisala notes:

> On one level we can view Aum as a social protest group.....Young people perhaps feel increasingly dissatisfied with the rewards offered for

long years of hard work in school and a drawn-out apprenticeship in the office with fewer opportunities for promotion than their fathers enjoyed. Perhaps this dissatisfaction has contributed to the contemporary interest in mystic and psychic abilities, forms of empowerment that many may see as more readily available than traditional forms of advancement. For some, dissatisfaction might also make apocalyptic ideas more appealing, offering a spectacular end to the status quo.[3]

Following the sarin gas attack of March 1995, many journalists and scholars, myself included, interviewed not only Aum members, but other young Japanese about their worldviews as well as their feelings about Aum. These interviews provide a good sampling of youthful voices that reflect the views of many younger Japanese in 1995-97. Thus, Aum and its members may serve as a legitimate "bellwether" to examine some aspects of alienation and religiosity in contemporary Japanese society.

People often turn to religion during periods of personal or societal hardship, change, or stress. The massive changes that have occurred in Japan since the Meiji Revolution over a century ago have led to three successive waves of New Religions (*shinshukyo*), all of which purported to provide answers for and to address the special needs of certain constituencies that felt left out or alienated from the progress of mainstream society.

The first wave of modern new religious activity began in the middle and later years of the Meiji period (1868-1912) as a result of the social changes and turbulence of the modernization process that had begun a generation earlier. These religions, which included Omotokyo, Tenrikyo, and Kurozumikyo, drew their greatest support from rural and urban areas most greatly affected by urbanization and industrialization.

The second wave of New Religions, which include such movements as the Soka Gakkai and Rissho Koseikai, began soon after World War II[4] and continued through the late 1960s and early 1970s. The founders of these religions were frequently Buddhist laymen with no close ties to any established sect who founded what became new lay Buddhist sects. They offered their own interpretations of Buddhist sacred books such as the Lotus Sutra and Buddhist teachings such of such figures as Nichiren[5]. These religions spoke to the very practical and concrete problems of less fortunate Japanese seeking to escape from such problems as poverty, disease, loneliness, and alienation from society. Some of these religious organizations implied that their more devoted followers could receive rapid material wealth and social success through deep faith and practice.

The third wave of New Religions began in the early 1970s and continues

Table 1: Major New Religions of Japan

Year Founded	Organization	Denomination	1994 Membership
Shinshukyo			
1814	Kurozumikyo	Shintoist	295,225
1838	Tenrikyo	Others	1,892,498
1859	Konkokyo	Shintoist	433,340
1892	Omotokyo	Shintoist	173,653
1913	Honmichi	Others	318,173
1919	Reiyukai	Buddhist	3,212,314
1924	Perfect Liberty	Others	1,234,457
1930	Seicho-no-ie	Others	872,198
1930	Soka Gakkai	Buddhist	8,030,000
1938	Risshokoseikai	Buddhist	6,545,950
Shinshinshukyo			
1948	Shinnyoen	Buddhist	816,920
1956	Kyuseishukyo	Others	177,264
1958	Unification Church	Others	463,991
1959	GLA	Others	16,384
1978	Agonshu	Buddhist	260,502
1979	Shinseikai	Others	71,340
1986	Kohuku-no-Kagaku	Others	unavailable
1987	Aum Shinrikyo	Others	10,000

SOURCE: *Japan Times Weekly*, international edition, 21-27 August 1995, p. 10. Soka Gakkai figure supplied by Soka Gakkai International in 1992.

through the present. By the 1980s Japan had achieved considerable economic wealth and most Japanese labeled themselves as middle class. Once Japan had achieved its earlier goal of prosperity, many people, especially younger Japanese and middle-aged women, began to lose a clear sense of purpose in their lives. This created a spiritual void that on occasion led to a fascination with mystical and occult phenomena often associated with "New Age" religious practices.[6]

Japan's Search for Spirituality

Recent studies indicate a decline in organized formalistic religious activity paralleled by a burgeoning interest in spirituality. New, often lay, religious movements and practices that promote independent and individual spiritual exploration have become immensely popular in the 1990s. Observers say that current economic uncertainty coupled with increased breakdown in family and community have left many, especially younger, Japanese feeling rootless and adrift.

Religious practice in Japan is a blend of many traditions. There is no dominating faith. Historically, Japanese have left little room for dogma. Faith is syncretic, often a combination of apparently contradictory beliefs. Buddhist, Shinto, and other traditions have become woven together in varying patterns depending on the individual or family. There is little consideration of reincarnation or different levels of reward after death. Instead, the focus is on happiness and gain in this lifetime.

This breakdown of traditional religious activity, the renewed search for less orthodox forms of spirituality, and the syncretic spiritual vista of many younger Japanese opens the way for new religious leaders and movements that cater to those citizens in search of some form of spiritual fulfillment. Asahara and Aum Shinrikyo before 1995 appeared to many Japanese as one of the more interesting counter-culture movements. Their syncretic religious ideas are not at all out of line with Japanese tradition.

Every generation has its dreamers, revolutionaries or misfits who for a variety of reasons opt out of mainstream society. Today there are many Japanese in their twenties and early thirties who find that they are neither emotionally nor intellectually suited to the rigors and pressures of Japan's postwar educational system and corporate life. Some of these younger Japanese quit the academic or corporate "rat race" to find companionship and solace in esoteric mysticism or religious practices of the "New New

Religions" (*shinshinshukyo*). They were joined by an impressive number of middle-aged people, especially women, who were seeking some meaning in life or an escape from the hard realities of modern life.[7] They are joined by a third group, young "blue-collar" workers who can find no satisfaction in their dull jobs and are anxious to escape all that is mundane in their lives.

Leading new religions of the 1970s-1990s include Agonshu, Aum Shinrikyo, and Sukyo Mahikari Kyodan. These *shinshinshukyo* apparently also attract some younger idealists who a generation earlier might have joined the leftist student movement. Many "young and angry" Japanese students of the 1960s and early 1970s developed strong anti-establishment values. They raised such questions as: "What does it mean to learn in a university?" "Is a university merely a factory which produces effective human resources for this economically normalized society?"[8] These students questioned the material values and the obsessive drive for wealth of mainstream Japanese society. They envisioned a more egalitarian society whose values were not solely tied to economic standards. Many of these student activists were attracted to Marxism.

Student activism declined sharply by the end of the 1970s. Many students developed an increasingly apathetic view of life and withdrew from the political arena. Some young Japanese began to focus their attention on the third wave of religious movements which "involved an esoteric mysticism centered around a charismatic guru."[9] Marxism lost its appeal and was replaced by a fascination for the occult and mystical superpower.

As Inagaki Hisakazu notes:

> [When] the rapid economic growth of postwar Japan began to decelerate..., many people found that simply acquiring material affluence did not satisfy. After Japan had joined the ranks of the great economic powers, people began to lose a clear sense of purpose in their lives. This created a void, both mentally and spiritually, that extended to the very depths of their souls. Some people undertook Yoga training, engaged in mystical meditation and explored the occult. They sought unusual, exotic experiences that would lift them above the humdrum routine of an affluent Japan....to find solace in esoteric mysticism or in the New Age Movement[10]

Some middle-aged Japanese felt similar or parallel frustrations. Workaholic men employed by companies that controlled virtually every aspect of their lives and much of their families' lives as well never had time at home. Some of their wives joined the younger generation in their search for meaning in life and compensation for the emptiness and loneliness they experienced each day. Some of them joined or had a genuine interest in Aum.[11]

Other younger Aum faithful come from more "blue-collar" backgrounds. Today many high school graduates who forsake a college education are having a difficult time finding satisfactory employment. The long economic recession of the 1990s has forced companies to reduce their staffs and to hire fewer people. The result is thousands of younger Japanese who are unemployed, underemployed or stuck in boring jobs that offer little fulfillment in life. When a religious movement such as Aum promises them special powers, an accepting community, and hope for happiness, a number of these youths will respond positively.

Religious movements such as Aum Shinrikyo appealed to the mystical, occult mentality that occupied the minds of increasing numbers of Japanese in the 1980s and 1990s. These younger Japanese reject the pragmatic utilitarian values of mainstream Japanese society in favor of a more humanistic worldview that seeks a better understanding of the "true meaning" of life. Youth looking for "salvation and recovery of soul" joined Aum because it promised them a prefabricated and easy solutions to their quest. Sadly, Asahara's highly publicized "Lotus Villages" – communes where devoted followers as well as Aum leaders lived—proved to be little more than potemkin-like mirages.

The fact that Japanese society does not have a support system for the marginalized creates unique opportunities for such religious groups as Aum Shinrikyo. They operate at a level far away from the mainstream and are generally shunned by most Japanese, but they are a genuine refuge for those living far beyond the confines of established life.

Chapter II
ഇാര
Aum Shinrikyo: Past And Present

Aum Shinrikyo has received a very negative image in the Japanese media. Its leader, Asahara Shoko, is often portrayed as an insane religious fanatic obsessed with power, money and sex. Aum is depicted as a murderous and very dangerous cult. Even a cursory study of Aum, however, indicates certain flaws in this imagery.

Religious Beginnings: Asahara's Early Life

Ian Reader, a long time student of Aum, asks whether it is necessary to have a dichotomous view of Asahara as both a true spiritual leader and as a murderous madman. Virtually all founders of new religions in postwar Japan are at least somewhat eccentric and Aum in its early years was in no way any more extraordinary than other *shinshinshukyo*. Asahara also has always been eccentric, but there is virtually no evidence in the early and mid-1980s that Aum would become so violent a decade later. There is clearly a shift in Asahara's temperament and world views across the spectrum from a position of optimism to one of deep pessimism and increased violence.

Asahara's true name is Matsumoto Chizuo — he adopted the pseudonym Asahara Shoko. He was born in 1955, the fourth son in a family of five brothers and two sisters. His father was a struggling and poorly educated *tatami* maker in a farming area of Yatsushiro, Kumamoto Prefecture, located on Japan's southern-most island of Kyushu. Congenitally afflicted with glaucoma, Asahara could see virtually nothing out of his left eye and had only thirty percent vision in his right eye.[1]

Asahara's father was too poor to provide for his children adequately, but he took advantage of his son's poor eyesight to send him to a special government-run boarding school for the blind. His father claimed that Asahara was totally blind so that he would qualify for a complete scholarship.[2] Midway through his first year at the local primary school, the six-year-old Asahara moved to the special school along with two of his brothers who were similarly impaired.[3] Asahara spent the next fourteen years, through primary school, middle school, high school, and a specialized course in acupuncture and moxibustion, living in school dormitories.

Asahara's life at school has received wide attention in the Japanese vernacular press. Most of these stories indicate that the future leader of Aum became a troublemaker and bully during his decade of study at the Kumamoto school. He used his visual abilities to gain advantages over his more severely impaired peers. He would do favors for them in exchange for small sums of money and their unswerving allegiance. There are reports that he was violent with a number of his cohorts when they "disobeyed" him and that many of the students feared his violent outbursts.

There were also times, however, when Asahara could be genuinely kind and even clownish. Some of his former peers told reporters that Asahara could be extremely warm and seemingly genuinely concerned about the welfare of others. Aum followers also remember this dichotomy in the behavior of their leader — instances of deep compassion interspersed with violent anger. One could never be sure of Asahara's mood on any given day. Apparently, Asahara has never been a stable person. There is every indication, however, that Asahara in general was a good student.

While in high school Asahara expressed a desire to attend the medical school at Kumamoto University and was then dismayed to find out that he did not qualify for the program because of his bad eyesight. Instead, Asahara completed a specialized course of study that qualified him to practice acupuncture and moxibustion and got a job as an acupuncturist in Kumamoto. By this time, however, he had decided to leave Kyushu and to establish a new life in Tokyo.

After his arrival in Tokyo in 1977, Asahara practiced acupuncture and moxibustion in Funabashi, Chiba Prefecture, near Tokyo,[4] worked as an acupuncturist and at the same time entered a "cram school" that was supposed to prepare him for the rigorous Tokyo University entrance exam. Acquaintances say that he spent much of his free time reading the revolutionary theoretical rhetoric of Mao Zedong and that he tried to learn how to read and write Chinese.[5] His hard work did not pay off, however, because he failed the entrance exam in 1977 and gave up the idea of a university education.[6]

One positive result of his study at the "cram" school was the encounter with another student, Ishii Tomoko, on a commuter train. Tomoko is the eldest daughter of school teachers in Kisarazu, Chiba Prefecture.[7] Asahara says that he fell in love with her immediately and told her at their second meeting that she would soon become his wife. She initially found him rather odd, but soon grew very fond of him. They were married in January, 1978.[8] The birth of their first daughter a year later forced Asahara to surrender his dreams of ever attending college and to earn money to support his young family. The Asaharas now have six children, four daughters and two sons, the last being born in 1994.[9]

The Asaharas continued to live in Funabashi, where he opened his own acupuncture and Chinese herbal medicine business, which he called the Chinese Medicine Asia Hall Pharmacy. Asahara's business was an immediate success—it is said that in less than three years be made a profit equivalent to several hundred thousand dollars.[10] He expanded his business in 1981 by opening the BMA Pharmacy, a store specializing in health foods and herbal medicines.[11] But it appears that Asahara was not satisfied with material success. He demonstrated a steadily increasing fascination with religion.

Asahara has said that he became interested in religion shortly after his marriage in 1978 because he was unable to cure some of his patients effectively through traditional medicine[12] He started to study traditional Chinese forms of divination leading ultimately to the practice of *sendo*, a set of traditional ascetic practices which he imagined gave him supernatural powers.[13] He also read the writings of Takahashi Shinji (1928-1976), the founder of GLA (God Light Association), a new religious group with spiritualist and New Age tendencies that in some respects resembles Asahara's own synthesis years later.[14] He also read the works of two other Japanese scholars of Buddhism, Nakamura Hajime and Masutani Fumio. Asahara was especially interested in their scholarship on early or "primitive" Buddhism in India. He was impressed that early Buddhists showed their great devotion by leaving their homes and old ways of life in favor of a life of rigorous meditation aimed at achieving Nirvana or enlightenment.[15]

A Brief History of Aum Shinrikyo

Although it is hard to make a distinction between the life of Asahara Shoko and the rise of Aum Shinrikyo, an introductory survey of the sect's history is necessary to give this study greater perspective.

Aum consisted of an inner group of up to 1100 renunciates[16] (shukkesha) who surrendered all of their material assets to Aum and lived a communal existence with the Master, and another 9,000 adherents who practiced Asahara's teachings at Aum meeting centers and who supported Aum in a variety of ways. Aum also operated various business enterprises including ramen (noodle) restaurants, bargain computer outlets and a busy publishing and media business. Aum's net worth at the height of its growth in the mid-1990s has been estimated as high as a billion dollars.

The rise and fall of Aum occurred in a remarkably short eight years (1987-95).[17] As it advanced in age it became more and more isolated and hostile not only to other religious groups but to society as a whole. Aum "increasingly and psychotically demonized outsiders, redrew protective boundaries even more tightly to prevent contamination by the impure world, and eventually even acquired arms...to defend the faithful, intimidate, and perhaps even eliminate real or supposed enemies."[18] When a handful of Aum Shinrikyo leaders planted the deadly nerve gas sarin in five subway cars on three lines in the Tokyo subway system on 20 March 1995, killing a dozen people and injuring 6,000 more, the sect was well known to some Japanese, but was not a "household word." Japanese were stunned to learn that a seemingly benign and small religious organization would use nerve gas for mass slaughter and would paralyze a whole city for reasons which even today are not entirely clear. What is clear is that the Aum attack gave the world a preview of a new form of terrorism in which chemical weapons have become a deadly threat.

Asahara's active religious practice began by 1980. Through the practice of yoga, he claimed in 1981 that he had experienced a Kundalini awakening, an arousal of vital or sexual energy which is said to transform body, mind, and emotions and lead to spiritual development. He joined the new religion Agonshu in 1981, but left the sect in 1984 to open his own yoga training center in Tokyo. Several of his earliest followers were Agonshu members who left the sect with him.

Asahara only attracted a few followers in the mid-1980s, but he gained notoriety because of his alleged levitation experiences and encounter with the Hindu god Shiva who is said to have commissioned him to build an ideal world, the kingdom of Shambhala, and his meetings in India in 1987 with various religious figures including the Dalai Lama, who Asahara claims anointed him as the Buddhist leader of Japan. Asahara named his organization Aum Shinsen no Kai in 1986 and renamed it Aum Shinrikyo in 1987.

Aum Shinrikyo formally applied for and eventually received religious corporation status in 1989 under the jurisdiction of the Tokyo metropolitan government. Aum's head office was in Tokyo, with branch offices in major cities throughout Japan and in Moscow, Bonn, Sri Lanka and New York. There was a general headquarters and training center in Fujinomiya, Shizuoka Prefecture and nearby land with a dozen buildings in the village of Kamikuishiki in Yamanashi Prefecture.[19] Aum claims to have had as many as 30,000 followers in Russia, but there was actually only a hardcore following of about 200. Other foreign branches had few if any members.

There are three identifiable stages in the evolution of Aum's worldview. During the first period which spanned the mid-1980s, Aum was little more than a yoga club whose members received yoga training under the tutelage of Asahara. Here Aum focused on the achievement of psychic powers leading to Kundalini enlightenment.

The second phase, which began with Asahara's first Indian pilgrimages (1986-87), saw an evolution towards various Buddhist concepts concerning enlightenment including a form of meditation as a means to liberation. Asahara's teachings focused on a mixture of Buddhist doctrines and yoga practices. He made a distinction between enlightenment (*satori*) and liberation (*gedatsu*) with liberation coming through the physical training of yoga and enlightenment arrived at through Buddhist practice (meditation).

During this phase Asahara emphasized Mahayana Buddhism with the goal of saving society as a whole from the coming Armageddon. He wanted to send Aum members to every country to convince the world of the validity of his teachings and to have everybody follow the path of non-violence. Aum's actions in the late 1980s focused on efforts to play a role in society rather than trying to destroy or supercede it.

The third phase of Aum's activity, which began in 1989, saw Aum develop an increasingly hostile and isolationist stance towards society. Asahara shifted Aum's doctrinal base away from a more inclusive Mahayana approach to one which represents his view of Vajrayana, an esoteric form of Indian Buddhism still popular in Tibet.

By the early 1990s Aum publications deal increasingly with the inevitability of an apocalyptic war. Asahara apparently became convinced that since the salvation of society as a whole was hopeless, everything must be done to preserve Aum even at the expense of society. It provided members with bomb shelters, air filters, and clothing to ward off electromagnetic radiation, and supplies of food and medicine so that they could survive the impending war. Aum built a chemical plant capable of producing substantial amounts of sarin gas, attempted with limited success to purchase advanced weapons and computers from the United States and Russia, and even stole weapons research data from a Mitsubishi plant near Tokyo.

It is not clear whether Aum intended to use the weapons and poi-son gas to defend itself from attacks by an increasingly hostile world or whether Aum intended to initiate Armageddon itself with a full-scale attack on Tokyo. But it is clear that Asahara became increasingly paranoid in his fear and hatred for the world outside Aum. Aum, in short, had become a very isolated world-rejecting sect.

Aum is famous for its two dozen or more murders, kidnapping, and other acts of violence, but there seems to be little correlation between Aum's alleged planned attacks on society and its more limited attacks on individuals or groups of individuals. Aum leaders were involved in two murderous incidents in 1989; several Aum officials killed a young member trying to escape the group while others murdered the family of Sakamoto Tsutsumi, a lawyer representing families of Aum members. Aum's violence was directed against perceived threats like Sakamoto, who threatened to publicly embarrass Aum, and judges in Matsumoto who might have rendered a negative decision against Aum in a law suit.[20] The sarin gas attack on the Tokyo subway was hastily planned when Aum heard of a massive police raid planned on its major facilities on 22 March 1995. Apparently Aum hoped to distract police by making them think that some other group such as the Soka Gakkai was the culprit.

Extensive manhunts and raids on Aum facilities in March, April and May of 1995 led to the arrest of the Aum hierarchy including Asahara and the recovery of mountains of evidence of Aum's misdeeds. Aum lost its status as a religious corporation and was declared bankrupt in late 1995-early 1996, but in 1997 the government failed in its attempt to totally suppress Aum through implementation of the 1952 Anti-Subversive Activities Law. The trials of Asahara and his other leading henchmen began in 1996 and still continue as of this writing.

Asahara as the Basis of Aum Theology

A thorough reading of Aum publications in both Japanese and English reveals a wide variety of religious teachings and jargon. Aum goes to great lengths to demonstrate that its theology is based on Buddhist principles, but Aum publications do make one factor abundantly clear: Asahara is portrayed as an "enlightened super-human" with divine powers at the level of Buddha and Jesus. Any Asahara devotee can improve his position in life (emancipation and enlightenment) and escape rebirth in human form only at the behest of Asahara himself — through his touch or blessing. There is simply no other path that offers so much to mankind.

Aum Shinrikyo is in effect a "One-Man Religion" focusing on the divinity and divine powers of Asahara himself. The closest equivalent might be the gurus in the Hindu tradition where a guru is a living human endowed with certain powers and/or knowledge that let him diminish or remove the karma of his disciples. Asahara, however, would claim that he is the "guru of gurus," endowed by the powerful Hindu god Shiva with the power to save humanity.

It is Asahara's "anointment" by Shiva that gives him most of his unique powers and wisdom. Asahara claims that Shiva "appeared" before him in late 1985 and told him that he, Asahara, was selected to lead mankind to salvation. Asahara's role is to be the human link between Lord Shiva and mere mortals. Asahara claimed to have a certain degree of divine powers including the awesome capacity to remove the evil karmas of people who, in effect, worship him.

Aum as a Religion

Aum Shinrikyo's belief structure and evolution parallel most other New Religions in Japan and Asahara's early career is quite similar to other New Religion founders.[21] Tokyo University Professor Shimazono Susumu writes:

> He [Asahara] emphasized intense ascetic practices for the achievement of (emancipation) and the teaching of a world-renouncing enlightenment. The tendency towards introspective faith, seen broadly in the New New Religions, is especially striking in Aum Shinrikyo.[22]

The downfall of Aum, Shimazono suggests, came from the very nature of its own interpretation of religious dogma and how one should respond to these teachings.

> The group fell into conflict with the surrounding society because of its push to rapidly increase the number of its world-renouncing members, adopting a style of proselytization common to previous New Religions aimed at mass mobilization. Rather than trying to resolve the tensions peacefully, Aum adopted an aggressive position, and, especially after 1989, its isolation deepened and headed towards violent introversion. Although its destructive violent nature only became evident in 1994, the roots of that violence were already present from the group's beginning. Elements that invite an eruption of violence, such as the conception of the human person as a mass of data that can be manipulated, a distorted understanding of Buddhism as justifying violence as a means and perceiving reality as an illusion, and an intense leader worship, were all present in Aum's universe of belief.[23]

The Rebirth of Aum

Many observers assumed that Aum Shinrikyo would die as a religious movement following the arrests of Asahara and other Aum leaders and the seizure of its assets. However, other Aum faithful have reorganized the movement and have brought in a surprising number of new members and money. Members pledge loyalty to Asahara and his teachings, but because their former leader can in no way communicate with them from his prison cell, Aum's new leaders are very much on their own.

Many of the current members belong to the sect before the March 1995 sarin gas incident. They abandoned the movement, but later returned because they felt that they had no other place to go. When interviewed by the Japanese media, current Aum members state that they live largely on the periphery of society after having been rejected by their families and employers upon discovering their links with Aum..

Police reports in early 1999 indicate a membership between 5,000 and ten thousand followers based around 15 offices and 100 places of meditation scattered nationwide. Aum has been reaching out to new members through the Aum page on the Internet. Virtual schools are conducted on the Internet for Aum children. Intensive recruitment is also carried out by Aum faithful in prestigious universities throughout Japan. Surveys indicate that most current members are in their twenties and thirties.

Aum has staged a strong financial recovery as well. Six Aum shops selling computers at discount rates report flourishing sales, which in 1997 exceeded four billion yen (around $US 29 million). Proceeds from seminars and lectures bring in additional revenue. There is very little indication, however, whether or not current members must make personal donations.

A recent documentary produced by Aum attracted large audiences in a downtown Tokyo cinema. The film attempts a far more sympathetic image of Aum. The documentary focuses on a twenty-eight-year-old member who is portrayed as being sincere and spiritual. Followers are depicted not as insane murderers, but earnest young men in search of spiritual learning. Aum spokesmen say the film portrays Aum as a mirror of Japanese society and that Aum is unique because it offers young Japanese a sense of spiritual mission and fulfillment, qualities they contend are lacking in contemporary Japanese life. The film also gives the impression that Aum is itself a victim.

There is no indication that the reconstructed Aum will resort to its former violent practices. The police are watching, but they report few if any suspicious activities. It appears that Aum will survive as a small peripheral movement attracting a handful of marginalized members of society.

Chapter III

ೲ

The Teachings of Asahara and Aum Shinrikyo

M y spiritual practice began in 1977.... I tried all kinds of practices such as Taoism, Yoga, Buddhism, incorporating their essence into my training. My goal was supreme spiritual realization and enlightenment. I continued the austere practices with Buddhist texts as my only resort. Finally, I reached my goal in the holy vibration of the Himalayas; I attained supreme realization and enlightenment. Thus my practice was completed, but what kind of state did I achieve as a result? I obtained absolute freedom, happiness and joy. Now I was qualified to enter Mahayana [i.e. Nirvana] when I died; I discovered the way to enter that state; I was free to leave my physical body anytime anywhere; I also acquired supernatural powers. In short, I could not have been happier. But my soul, my deeper self, was not satisfied. How should I express it—I could not bear the fact that only I was happy and the other people still in the world of suffering. I began to think: "I will save other people at the sacrifice of my own self. I have come to feel it is my mission. I am to walk the same path as Buddha Sakyamuni."[1]
—Asahara Shoko in the premier issue of Aum Shinrikyo's journal, *Maha=yana* in 1987.

A fundamental task confronting any coherent religious movement is the interrelated definition of some form of salvation together with the articulation of a rigorous methodology by which to attain that higher state.

Religious founders and leaders typically diagnose the ills and evils of the human condition and then offer normative prescriptions. Both the critical diagnosis and the theoretical prescription change as a systematic organic religion evolves and grows. Japan's Aum Shinrikyo and its founder, Asahara Shoko, provide salient examples of this complex, evolutionary process.

Aum's theology, although it was quite eclectic, has its origins in the Buddhist, Shinto and folk religious traditions of Japan and has strong parallels with some of the other *shinshinshukyo* that developed in Japan after the mid-1970s. Aum also made practical utilization of aspects of Hindu and esoteric Buddhist cosmology and practice:

> The concept of a path towards higher consciousness via a variety of stages marked by various initiations which form a crucial ritual practice; the importance of the spiritual leader or guru as guide and as the source of initiation; and the importance of ascetic practices—yoga, meditation, and renunciation of the world. It also expressed various aspects of contemporary Japanese religion...such as millenialism allied to a strong critique and, ultimately, rejection of contemporary materialism, along with a deep reverence for the charismatic powers of its leader and his ability to guide followers to the enlightenment.[2]

Asahara and Aum also made an effort to mix Indian and Japanese motifs in its objects of worship (which included the Hindu god Shiva), the clothing of Asahara and other Aum leaders, and the Indian names given to longtime members. Unlike many other new religions in Japan which seek to strongly identify themselves with the Japanese nation, Aum seemed to have very few nationalistic leanings. Aum regarded Japanese society as an oppressive and even evil force that sought to discredit or even destroy Asahara's band. Aum had to somehow destroy or circumvent Japanese society before the millenium could come about.[3]

Hindu practices and motifs—in addition to devotion to the god Shiva—include a strong focus on yoga accompanied by certain physical and spiritual austerities which are said to bestow extraordinary mental and physical powers on devoted practitioners.[4]

Aum's theology is strongly influenced by various aspects of Buddhism. Although some scholars have correctly indicated that Aum misinterpreted and misrepresented various aspects of Buddhist doctrine[5], Aum defined itself as a "Buddhist" movement. Aum's cosmology, practices and imagery are based on its view of Buddhism. It reflects Buddhist ideas on transmigration, rebirth, the sinful nature of the world, human suffering in this life, and a path toward better rebirths and enlightenment for the devotee through such spiritual disciplines as renunciation and meditation. Asahara had a special interest in Tibetan Buddhism. He carried on some form of correspondence with the Dalai Lama, met him on several occasions, and distributed pictures of them together in various Aum publications.[6]

Aum even added some Christian imagery into its eclectic world-view. Asahara's millenialist ideas were derived from his readings of the Revelations of St. John and its depictions of the Apocalypse. Asahara believed that he was the savior foretold by Nostradamus and strongly identified himself as the Christ[7] who had come to save the world but who would have to sacrifice his life to complete his mission.[8]

The Basic Message

Aum's message to the world was not unlike those of other Japanese new religions. Society is in decline because of a fundamental decay in spirituality. Japanese are too focused on money and materialistic vanities to realize that they are heading towards total collapse—destruction in a global war. The only escape is through the leadership and teachings of Asahara and Aum. When Japanese accepted Asahara as their leader (guru), Japan would become a realm of peace, harmony and spirituality and spread these values to the rest of the world bringing about an era of global peace.

Aum's theology is also based on the idea that the world is predominantly sinful and that life is primarily a process of suffering. One may escape from suffering through spiritual practice and find a greater sense of reality in such spiritual practices as meditation rather than in the mundane world.

> Thus Aum, in contrast to the positivistic attitudes of most Japanese new religions, which offer their followers the potential for realization, success and achievement in this world, not only asserted a critical and antithetical view of society and of Japanese materialism, but asserted the importance of withdrawing from it to practice austerities. This apparently idealistic rejection of wealth and materialism in favor of spiritual progress through asceticism, yoga and meditation attracted to it young, idealistic people who were dissatisfied or disillusioned by the materialism, stifling conformity, rigid structures and competitiveness of Japanese society.[9]

Asahara claimed that his enlightenment had brought him extraordinary powers (*siddhis*) including levitation, clairvoyance, and the ability to break free from the cycle of birth and death into Nirvana.[10] Asahara promised similar benefits to his faithful as well as assurance that they alone would survive the impending Armageddon.

Asahara proclaimed himself to be the ultimate Buddhist savior, but, as Richard Young notes, Asahara and Aum lacked many of the basic ingredients of true Buddhism including "ethical training and a life of virtue based on, for instance, the Noble Eight-Fold Path of the Theravada that the Master professed to follow. That is to say, there was in Aum a pathbreaker, but no path markers for others to follow after he was gone."[11]

The Evolution of Aum's Ideology

Every new religion experiences considerable change as it matures and Aum Shinrikyo is no exception. Aum is famous for the catastrophic millenialist bent it displayed in the mid-1990s, but in its initial stages it was a small benign movement with an optimistic view of life and its role in society. It early focus was on the salvation of individual members, but it soon developed a Mahayana approach that sought the salvation of the whole of humanity and its own inclusion into the mainstream of Japanese life. By the early 1990s, however, Aum developed a rejectionist attitude towards society and had virtually declared war on Japan.

Aum's worldview was based on the idea that society is sinful and that life is a difficult process of suffering. It emphasized the importance of escaping this suffering through strict spiritual practice and of "finding reality not in the world of substance, but in spiritual disciplines such as meditation."[12] Aum's philosophy and actions ran contrary to the traditional positivistic attitudes of most traditional and new religions of Japan which are often world-affirming and which offer followers the potential for the realization of happiness and material success here and now. Aum asserted both a critical and antithetical view of society and of Japanese materialism and taught the need to withdraw from society to practice austerities. This seemingly idealistic rejection of wealth, materialism and the supposed "emptiness" of modern Japanese society in favor of spiritual progression through asceticism, yoga and meditation attracted a group of young, idealistic people who were dissatisfied with the apparent material-ism, conformity, rigid structures and competitiveness of modern Japanese society.[13]

Aum developed a form of millenialism that stressed that the world can be transformed from the crisis-ridden, polluted, warlike and materialistic world we live in today into a place of love, joy, peace, abundance and harmony. But its view of what the world would look like when the millenium was achieved was vague. Aum's vision involved the advent of a messiah, Asahara, and the creation of a superior society where people with superior powers and intelligence would live for a long time.

Yoga

Asahara initially turned to Hindu traditions to lead mankind to salvation. His Aum Shinsenno-kai was concerned primarily with practicing yoga and gaining extraordinary powers (such as Asahara's alleged levitation experiences)as evidence that one had attained certain spiritual stages of enlightenment

Asahara subscribed to very basic principles of Hindu tradition in his Yoga practice including the very simple principle that in every human being there is a source of divine energy. The Sanskrit word for this source of energy is Kundalini. Kundalini is in two states: the dormant state, and the active, aroused, or awakened state. When this source is dormant, a person leads an incomplete, unfulfilled life. One's understanding of the universe is restricted, and everything is perceived and interpreted according to a limited capacity. On the other hand, when the source is active, progress is rapid on the path of spiritual evolution. One realizes the full potential of body and mind, attains inner peace, harmony and integration, and ultimately experiences the sublime truth of unity in diversity—the fact that all life is one and is bound by that divine power called love. The purpose of Yoga is to awaken this source of energy if it is dormant, or to intensify the activity if it is already awakened. Thus, Asahara's view of Yoga is said to be a direct method for spiritual evolution and as such its importance is obvious. A side benefit of the awakened Kundalini is the automatic healing of diseases of the body and mind by the divine energy.[14]

Asahara claimed that powerful Yoga masters such as himself have the power to awaken the aspirant's *Kundalini* by a transfer of his or her energy to the aspirant. This process, known as *Shaktipat,* activates the dormant *Kundalini* and is like lighting a candle with one that is already lit and glowing. *Shakti* means power or energy in Sanskrit, and *pat* means transfer.

The concept of *Kundalini* played a very important role in Asahara's thinking in the early stages of his religious development in the mid-1980s. According to the physiology of *raja yoga*, which Asahara studied, *Kundalini* is a huge reserve of spiritual energy situated at the base of the spine. When the *Kundalini* is aroused, it is said to travel up the spine through six centers o conscious-ness (*chakras*), reaching the seventh, the center of the brain. As it reaches the higher centers, it produces various degrees of enlightenment.

Asahara's teachings at this phase centered on the release of *Kundalini* energy through Yoga to allow the practitioner to achieve Emancipation [*gedatsu*] or liberation from suffering in this world ("transcending life and death"). It is apparent that the "awakening of *kundalini*" and its liberating effects on the practitioner were the pillars of his practice until at least 1986.

The successful practitioner of Yoga will move up through stages that reflect ecstasy, joy, calmness and ease before finally achieving *Samadhi*, the ultimate liberation from suffering, the stage between life and death. Yoga, however, did have its limitations because, according to Asahara, it could only lead one through the stage of ecstasy. He later announced that he had encountered the higher stages when he turned to Tibetan Buddhism

The Role of Shiva

By 1985 Asahara began to claim various extraordinary experiences such as levitation and to exhibit an awareness of his qualities as a charismatic leader.[15] He also claimed that while engaging in the practice of a homeless monk and performing prostrations at Miura Beach in Kanagawa Prefecture near Tokyo, the Hindu god Shiva suddenly appeared before Asahara and told him that he was therewith appointed "Abiraketsu no Mikoto." Asahara tells us that this means that he is "the god of light who leads the armies of the gods" and that Shiva has appointed him to create an ideal society made up of those who have attained psychic powers, a society known as the Kingdom of Shambhala.[16] Later some Aum members suggested that Asahara's identification himself with Shiva had enhanced their leader's authority significantly in their eyes.

Mahayana Buddhism

With rare exceptions scholars have paid little attention to the "Mahayana Phase" of Aum's development, which culminated in 1987-88 with the publication of Asahara's book, *Inishieshon* [Initiation].[17] This neglect is unfortunate; a full appreciation of Aum's ideology in the mid-1990s requires examination of the movement's earlier intellectual influences and formulations.

The shift towards Mahayana marked a shift of Aum from a rather introverted group of people who were seeking their own happiness, a mark of Hinayana Buddhism, to a broader social view that encompassed a more social vision. Starting in 1987, Aum sought to open itself more to society, to become a modern *sangha* whose aim was to lead the world past its current state of suffering to greater happiness and peace. Mahayana, according to Asahara, represented practice leading not only to one's own enlightenment, but to the "ultimate freedom and happiness of others."[18]

One of the traditional figures in Mahayana Buddhism is the Bodhisattva, a being who has overcome his own suffering, but who postpones his departure from society to devote himself unselfishly to the salvation of other less fortunate beings. Asahara regarded himself as a Bodhisattva who had found the path to enlightenment himself and who now saw it as his duty to sacrifice his own happiness to bring similar blessings to others.

During the late 1980s Asahara and Aum stressed that its goal followed the Mahayana tradition of the salvation of all of humanity both here and now. He described three types of salvation: Saving others from the suffering of illness, bringing true happiness to the world, and leading all people to *satori* and *gedatsu*. "Only after emancipation and enlightenment are combined can we save others. To lead people to the world of true freedom, true happiness and true pleasure, this is the salvation we are aiming at."[19]

Asahara wrote that suffering for others has a salvific function:

> When you are suffering, your past bad deeds are being washed off, which means you can be reborn in a higher world in your next life. But when you take your joy as joy, you are losing your merits, which means you will be reborn in one of the three miserable realms. In the next step, if you take away the suffering of others, it is the practice of Mahayana. This is the most wonderful practice....If each one of you becomes a sun lighting up everyone around you and connects everyone around you to the truth, an incomparable world will be formed.[20]

Inishieshon presents a mixture of Buddhist doctrines and yoga practices. What is important is the addition of Buddhist doctrines to Aum's agenda with "meditation on sundry Buddhist concepts taking precedence over the practice of yoga." Asahara also makes an important distinction between Enlightenment *(satori)* and Emancipation *(gedatsu)*. These two terms parallel a doctor's diagnosis of an illness and his prescription for a cure. One's Enlightenment is the realization of the fact that there is a problem; Emancipation is the means by which one overcomes the problem. Enlightenment is achieved through meditation while Emancipation comes through the physical training of yoga.[21]

Asahara regarded himself as an enlightened being with the unique power and ability to save the world. He held an eschatological view of the world, declaring that mankind is doomed because of the overwhelming presence of evil and the lack of a spiritual leader to lead man to a better world. He felt that the solution to man's evil ways can be found in Buddhism and that the absence of true Buddhist belief, practice and leadership is the chief cause of human misery.

Asahara claims to have found both Enlightenment and Emancipation in India during a 1987 visit when he met with numerous religious figures, including the Dalai Lama.[22] According to Asahara's own version of the meeting with the Dalai Lama, Asahara recalls the Tibetan leader telling him:

> "Dear friend, look at the Buddhism of Japan today. It has degenerated into ceremonialism and has lost the essential truth of the teachings. As this situation continues, Buddhism will disappear from Japan. Something needs to be done, and you should spread real Buddhism there. You can do that well. If you do so, I shall be very pleased and it will help me with my mission." He added, "You can do that well, because you are a *Bodhichitta*...." A *Bodhichitta* means the mind of a Buddha. Since I have determined to work for salvation as a Mahayana Buddha, it is my great joy that such a great person as His Holiness said to me, "You have a *Bodhichitta*.[23]

Asahara in publishing this quote has hit upon a traditional theme in Japanese Buddhist history—that the evil running rampant through contemporary society is caused by the fact that people have forgotten the true meaning of Buddhism and that the practice of Buddhism has degenerated into "ceremonialism." Peace, happiness and harmony will prevail only when people understand and practice the original teachings of the Buddha Shakyamuni. Asahara claims to be the Buddhist messiah of Japan, appointed the country's savior by the Dalai Lama.[24]

Asahara adopts the traditional Buddhist premise that the known world and, indeed, life itself is full of suffering. His view of the path to enlightenment is "world-denying" in so far as its practice ignores the ways and pleasures of the world in its promotion and disciplined focus on the individual's "heart and mind."[25] Enlightenment, however, is not the final answer—it is but a stepping stone to the realization that we cannot find genuine freedom and happiness within the confines of everyday life and so must seek spiritual emancipation from the artificial structures and dynamics of the material world.

Shimazono Susumu argues that Aum encountered severe problems in defining "absolute freedom and happiness" in 1987 and 1988 and that these doctrinal problems presented Aum with a major, subsequent difficulty in leading faithful disciples to the achievement of a world-detached state.[26] Aum, i.e., Asahara, was looking for what one in the West calls a statement of mind-body duality that would be amenable to synthetic-spiritual transformation. Asahara embraced the dual disciplines of Jnana-Kundalini yoga, writing: "If we pursue happiness logically [Jnana yoga], we attain enlightenment. If we pursue happiness physically [Kundalini yoga], we attain emancipation. When you attain both and combine them, you are in a supreme condition."[27]

During the late 1980s Asahara and Aum stressed that its goal followed the Mahayana tradition of the salvation of all of humanity both here and now. He described three types of salvation: Saving others from the suffering of illness, bringing true happiness to the world, and leading all people to *satori* and *gedatsu*. "Only after emancipation and enlightenment are combined can we save others. To lead people to the world of true freedom, true happiness and true pleasure, this is the salvation we are aiming at."[28]

An Aum recruiting pamphlet published in 1988 describes Asahara's dream of bringing happiness to all mankind:[29]

> This kingdom (Shambhala), ruled by the god Shiva, is a world where only those souls which have attained the complete truth of the universe can go. In Shambhala, the ascetic practices of messianic persons have made great advances in order to lead souls to *gedatsu* (emancipation) and save them. Master Asahara has been reborn from there into the human world so that he might take up his mission as messiah. Therefore, the Master's efforts to embody truth throughout the human world has been sanctioned by the great will of the God Shiva.
>
> Let us take a look, however, at the situation in Japan and the world. Clearly we face a very dangerous situation, due to the rapid increase of egoism. Master Asahara's prophecies, such as a worsening of the trade friction between the United States and Japan, an increase in defense spending, and abnormalities in the Fuji volcanic region and the Pacific

Plate have already proved true.

If we allow the demonic energy to increase, it will be extremely difficult to prevent the slide towards a nuclear war at the end of the century. For that reason Aum Shinrikyo's plan to transform Japan into Shambhala was presented. This plan was without equal in its scope, as it wants to extend Aum's sacred sphere throughout all of Japan, making Japan the base for the salvation of the whole world by fostering the development of multitudes of holy people. This plan cannot be realized without the help of our believers. Please come and join us!

Wouldn't you like to help build a society based on truth, and help more and more souls to live the life of truth, leading to *gedatsu* and life in a higher world? Wouldn't you like to help the world avoid disaster and build a future of happiness? Let us combine our efforts, and translate into action the great will of the God Shiva and our guru, Master Asahara. The plan to transform Japan into Shambhala is the first step towards making the whole world Shambhala. And your participation in this plan will result in great merit and lead you to a higher world.

The pamphlet provided an "Outline of the Plan," which included details for the establishment of a type of commune called "The Lotus Village."

This means the construction of an Aum village, so that everyone can live a life founded on truth. We will build a completely independent society, providing everything from clothing, food, and housing to a place for religious practice, medical and educational facilities, weddings and funerals, and opportunities for employment. We will also establish facilities for medical, scientific and agricultural research, so that it will become a place to create a culture of truth.

Asahara concludes *Supreme Initiation* with an apocalyptic vision of the world. He predicts that Japan will rearm itself by 1993, and there will be a nuclear world war at some point between 1999 and 2003 that will destroy most of humanity. But this catastrophe, Asahara carefully qualified, could be averted IF Aum had a branch in every major country tutored by an emancipated spiritual leader or, at a minimum, by someone enlightened. Such national-spiritual leaders, Asahara opined, will preach against all forms of violence. Only if and when a majority of the world's peoples follow the Aum doctrine of emancipation, can we hope to avoid World War III.

Robert Kisala critically notes of Asahara's argument:

The salvation indicated here does not necessarily depend on mystic or spiritual agencies, but rather on the fact that the world can be convinced of the truth and follow a path of non-violence, led by Aum. Even if the predicted war cannot be avoided, however, the followers of Aum's practice will be able to leave their bodies behind and enter into the Astral World...described as the Clear Light. Clearly this vision is still in its germinal stage. However, it does introduce one of the major themes elaborated on in later developments—the survival of those who have attained supernatural powers through Aum's practice.[30]

At this point in its development, Aum was dedicated to the pursuit of Mahayana's optimistic approach to the salvation of the world. Aum was vigorous in its advocacy of non-violence and universal Buddhahood which is realizable if we follow the ideal king of Shambala, who, of course, is none other than Asahara himself.

By 1990, however, Asahara seems to have given up on the Mahayana approach of trying to save society through social action and active proselytization. He no longer seemed inclined to change the world by "scattering Buddhas"[31] and interacting with others. Instead, feelings of pessimism, hopelessness, desperation and even powerlessness seem to have overwhelmed Asahara. He apparently decided that the only way to escape further trouble was to practice more strictly and to lock himself and his closest followers into carefully protected communes that were totally shut off from the outside world. "The opening up to society, the detour of Mahayana, had proved to be a blind alley."[32] He told his faithful:

> We don't know what to do with this society, with this world of ours. But it is true that this small group is growing, that it is becoming a power. This power will grow to protect us; if we put our forces together, we will have the power to protect ourselves. That is what we are going to do now. Nuclear shelters and other protective facilities [have to be built]....Practice much harder than you are practicing now, and sublimate yourself to the stage where you are ready to die at any time.[33]

One factor that greatly worried Asahara at the start of the 1990s was the small size—3,000 members at the time—of his movement. Massive recruitment, raising money from existing and new recruits, and halting the defection of members became the Aum chief's top goals. If Aum were to grow from a tight nucleus at the "Lotus Village" level into a "city" with the capacity to send representatives around the world, massive recruitment was a must. The need to expand Aum remained an obsession of Asahara's through the 1995 sarin incident and caused a great deal of pressure to be placed on the membership.[34]

Aum's Political Debacle

Aum's last attempt at Mahayana-like inclusion in society was its surprising entry in the February 1990 Japanese general election. The very fact that Aum members including Asahara attempted to win power through politics indicates that Asahara still thought that society could be saved if its members won positions in the Diet.

Asahara and Aum Shinrikyo's participation in the February 1990 general election for the Lower House of the Japanese Diet is one of the most interesting and entertaining episodes in the nation's modern electoral history. Asahara along with twenty-five of his close disciples organized a political party, the Shinri-to (Truth Party), and campaigned with considerable energy throughout the country.

Aum's participation in politics is not an anomaly in Japanese history. The fact that Asahara and his followers sought high office stems from a tradition in Japanese society that strongly links religion and other aspects of society. Americans have a long tradition of the separation of church and state, but such an idea is less emphasized in Japan. On the contrary, Japan has a long tradition that links politics and religion together under the divine authority of the emperor. A number of new religious organizations have been quite active in Japanese politics in the postwar era.

Scholars have presented other motives for Aum's quixotic bid for power. Shoko Egawa, a journalist who has followed Aum since the late 1980s, suggests that the whole operation was no more than a public relations gambit for Aum. She believes that the real goal being an increase in membership and with it an increase in donations—and an attempt to win more public recognition and respect.[35] If public relations was the goal, then the campaign was a disaster. Aum candidates campaigned in white robes and Aum followers gathered in front of subway stations and danced about wearing huge papier-mâché heads of Asahara while singing the Shinri-to campaign song which translates in English as:

Shoko, Shoko, Shoko-Shoko-Shoko, Asahara Shoko
Shoko, Shoko, Shoko-Shoko-Shoko, Asahara Shoko

Japan's Shoko, the world's Shoko, the earth's Shoko, Shoko, Shoko

He rises now, shining brilliantly
Let's put ourselves in the hands of our youthful hero
To protect our Japan, we need his strength
Shoko, Shoko, Asahara Shoko

Asahara's campaign turned into one embarrassing joke—a public display of twisted idolatry and mind control that revolted the public. The Shinri-to did have some campaign themes including the end of the national consumption tax and an appeal to utopian socialism ("Freedom, equality, and benevolence for every being, especially for every Japanese")[36] and it is said to have spent a phenomenal $7 million on the race. Sadly for Aum, its candidates went down to humiliating defeats. Asahara himself only garnered 1,783 votes in a district where a half million ballots were cast. Asahara got even fewer votes than one of his younger colleague, Fumihiro Joyu, who got over 1,800 votes. Asahara himself admitted that "It was a complete loss."[37]

Another possible motivation for Asahara's electoral bid was his lifelong dream of becoming a successful politician and a political leader of Japan. His childhood dream of studying at Tokyo University seems to have been motivated by a deep desire to use a Todai degree as the ticket to the political world. He never achieved admission to any university, but perhaps he felt that his growing fame as the leader of a new and rapidly growing religious group would be his ticket to office.

Asahara's pathetic political campaign drained millions of dollars from Aum's coffers, encouraged a number of long-term members to quit the movement, and made both the movement and its leader the object of considerable public derision. Asahara was himself totally embarrassed and humiliated by the campaign.

Aum's defeat and Asahara's increasingly pessimistic views of society's propensity to accept him as its true savior from the impending doom of Armageddon led him to compare himself to Jesus Christ. He was the "lamb of God" who had come to save at least a small remnant of society, but destined himself to be sacrificed for all humanity.[38] He quotes the Bible (I Peter: 18-20) in his 1992 book, *Declaring Myself the Christ*, to prove that he is in fact the Messiah:

> You know that you were ransomed from the futile ways inherited from your ancestors, not with perishable things like silver and gold, but with the precious blood of Christ, like that of a lamb without defect or blemish. He was destined before the foundation of the world, but was

revealed at the end of the ages for your sake....[39]

Let us look at the situation of Aum Shinrikyo now. When did the slaying happen to Aum? It began when Aum got involved in the election and declared freedom, equality, and benevolence for every being, especially for the Japanese, spreading the hospice movement and campaigning against the consumption tax at the same time. Since then, just like a Lamb who was slain, Aum has sacrificed its honor and position in society for the sake of its teaching.

The Shift to Vajrayana Buddhism

This Mahayana stance is strikingly different from the pessimistic posture Aum adopted in 1989 and 1990. At this time Asahara concluded that Armageddon was a necessary prelude for the cleansing of the world of all wickedness through the medium of the destructive effects of total nuclear war. This self-initiated Armageddon, Asahara now believed, would lead to the creation of the kingdom of Shambala and the "post-apocalyptic rule of enlightened Aum followers.[40]

As noted earlier, the key element in this changed world view is Aum's 1989 adaptation of its particular version of the esoteric, "bad-karma" Vajrayana Buddhism, an esoteric form of Indian Buddhism later popularized in Tibet which holds that the use of "mystical symbols, gestures and chants are the most effective means of achieving advanced spiritual states, and aims at the achievement of psychic powers."[41] This form of Buddhism originated and flourished in India from the fifth century onwards with the decline of the Gupta Empire, when many Indians developed an interest in the cults of feminine deities "and in the practice of magico-religious rites, which were believed to lead to salvation or to superhuman power."[42]

Another aspect of Vajrayana Buddhism that clearly interested Asahara is the role of the *Siddha*, a religious master whose spiritual realization is said to be so profound that he has power over the phenomenal world, including the power of levitation, or, in extreme cases, the power to fly or to stop the movement of the sun. The *siddha* is also a powerful religious figure and teacher with the power to save the world. Asahara boasts in one Japanese-language publication that he does indeed possess such power— that he is imbued with the sacred capacity to permit him and his followers to survive Armageddon.[43] Indeed, Asahara now began teaching that he as an enlightened guru could bring *gedatsu, satori*, and salvation to devotees through the energy generated by his secret knowledge and ritual practice.[44]

Asahara interpreted Vajrayana in a number of ways, including those which he felt gave him the right to commit a number of evil acts, including murder. He proposed the hypothetical example of a person who after having led a virtuous life accumulating enough merit enters heaven. He then introduces a person who in early life accumulates merit, but who later in life becomes lazy and is in grave danger of acquiring bad karma. If that person is killed before acquiring bad karma, he will be saved and his murderer will gain merit by saving his victim from the torment of bad karma. One finds this perverse logic when Asahara congratulated his followers who had spearheaded the subway gas attack in Tokyo—the dead commuters and subway officials had been killed for their own good, spared the torment that a declining lifestyle might have brought them.

Asahara's shift to Vajrayana brought with it a very different perception of his and Aum's worldview and relationship with society. The desire to build peaceful "Lotus villages" was replaced by an increasingly paranoiac view of the outside world. Rather than building a better world for all people, Aum began to see the world as so corrupt that salvation for more than a few superhumans was impossible. Aum's goal became self-protection from a contaminated world.

Aum began to display several elements that made it rather unique in the history of Japanese new religious movements. He increasingly insisted on the absolute devotion and obedience of the disciple to the leader thus creating a direct physical and mental bond between guru and student. Renunciation, increasingly severe ascetic practices and the salvic physical energy became the only way to salvation.[45]

Aum's murder of innocent citizens and utter disregard for Japanese law has shocked a nation noted for its respect for law and tradition, but an equally disturbing factor is the callous, ruthless efficiency of the organization that they created. Aum leaders preached that the only hope for their survival was in isolation, groupism and their own brand of self-reliance. Members ceded not only their entire family fortunes, but also their very identity to the group. The faithful were expected to work tirelessly and unquestioningly for what Aum's leaders assured them was best for the group and, by extension, best for them.

Aum members learned that the outside world consisted of a satanic force that neither understood nor tolerated their unique and mystical religion and that outsiders were determined to destroy it. Aum leaders constantly warned of the danger posed by these outsiders and fostered a siege mentality that gave them strict control over every aspect of their lives. Any questioning of Aum's teachings and Asahara's authority was tantamount to treason.

This siege mentality together with the belief that outsiders were willing to use violence to destroy the sect apparently convinced Aum members that they should respond violently in self-defense. Thus, brutality, abduction, confinement, flagrant violations of human rights and utter disregard for the norms of a civil society became acceptable practices in the name of self-defense.

The structure of the Aum community became focused on the absolute authority of Asahara who was now worshipped as an awesome superhuman entity. Near the end of his reign, Aum publications describe Asahara as "the spirit of supreme truth: the most holy, Master Asahara Shoko" and in descriptions of his own government as "Sacred / divine emperor or king."[46] The lines of loyalty were between Asahara and each individual member; horizontal ties between members were weak, even non-existent. Ascetic practices such as meditation and long periods of isolation only enhanced the individual's dependence on Asahara.

Asahara steadily increased the number of initiatory rituals in which his powers were transferred to his followers, thus enabling them to rise higher in the spiritual world. These practices emphasized the physical powers inherent in Asahara's body and the need of the practitioner to come into physical contact with his body or body parts and waste to absorb his energy. Thus, Reader notes, "Eventually a whole series of initiatory rituals involving Asahara's physical traces developed, each costing his disciples increasing amounts of money. Thus his bath water could be drunk to imbibe his spiritual energy, and his blood imbibed to absorb his DNA through which his spiritual forces were taken into his disciples' bodies."[47] There are also accounts of former members who insist that they were fed hallucinogenic drugs in the water or blood they drank. Some followers who experienced extraordinary sensations when consuming these liquids were at the time convinced of Asahara's extraordinary powers.

Aum increased Asahara's authority and his followers' dependence on him through a systematic program of mind control, violence and drugs. Aum faithful had to listen to hours of tapes containing Asahara's teachings interspersed with soft music and other material. They were fed drugs which weakened their resistance, induced prolonged periods of hallucinations, and convinced them that they could see the many spiritual realms described by Asahara in his sermons and essays. Their food had little nutritional value, bringing on even more weakness and illness. If some of the stronger members tried to escape, they were severely punished. A few successful escapees were kidnapped and brought back to Aum centers where they were held prisoner or, on rare occasions, killed. When police raided Aum facilities in late March, 1995, television viewers were treated to the ugly sight of emaciated Aum renunciates in states of near collapse due to their terrible diets and extreme practices of asceticism.

The ill-treatment of Aum members near the end evolved from Asahara's growing belief that extreme asceticism was the only way to liberation and survival and that they had to be *made* to do ascetic practices for their own good. One example is Aum's belief that through lengthy breathing exercises the disciple could sharply reduce or even stop his intake of oxygen, which was necessary if they were to live for long periods in small underground shelters with limited supplies of oxygen.

Asahara describes various alleged experiments with members to show that unlike normal humans, they have developed the ability to survive with little or no oxygen intake. In the case of member Maha Khema Seitashi, "measurements were made in a completely air-tight chamber submerged in water for approximately 20 hours. Respiratory cessation for a continuous 11 hours and 20 minutes was recorded....As we can see from the results of these experiments, the oxygen consumption of practitioners is always low and those in an advanced stage of practice can actually stop breathing for a long period of time at will. This state is called samadhi, the ultimate state of meditation. The influence of radiation would be very small or non-existent upon these kinds of practitioners."[48]

Armageddon

The concept of Armageddon, the idea of the total destruction of the existing world and the emergence of a new higher order, is a familiar theme in many religions including Zoroastrianism, Judaism, Christianity and Islam. The story is always quite simple—a struggle between evil and good, the final war, and the eventual victory of good over evil. In Zoroastrianism, the final war is waged between the God of Light, Ahura Mazda, and the God of Darkness, Ahriman. The war ends with the victory of Ahura Mazda and the emergence of the Kingdom of God. The Christian version of Armageddon is chronicled in the sixteenth chapter of Revelation where Satan and the forces of evil meet their demise. Apocalyptic writing is found in Japanese

Buddhism with the concept of *mappo*, which literally means "the end of dharma, or Buddhist law."

Aum's progressive doctrinal pessimism was premised on and paralleled by Asahara's crystallizing perception of both the evil nature of the material world and the increasingly urgent need for the faithful to withdraw from it. This home-grown pessimism was tellingly and ironically accompanied by mounting incidents of conflict between the faithful and the outside world.[49] and by a hardening radical attitude that Aum is divinely destined to play a role in fostering apocalyptic events, thereby securing the inevitable higher order for the true believers. Thus, prior to its terrorist attack on Tokyo subway commuters in March of 1995, Aum Shinrikyo had redefined as a radical, world-rejecting religious movement adamantly opposed to the substance and structures of modern society.[50] In less than a decade, its leader had enunciated an apocalyptic vision predicting the imminent moment when the corrupt world will destroy itself and a new utopian society of more perfect beings will emerge.[51] Asahara's worldview holds that the forces of evil will destroy themselves, together with their evil karma, before the idealistic Buddhist domain of "Shambhala" emerges.[52] Aum's self-defining shift from an optimistic to a doctrinally pessimistic movement came between 1989 and 1990 when Aum stopped seeing itself as a Mahayana Buddhist movement and adopted its own interpretive version of Vajrayana Buddhism. When Mahayana dominated its teachings, Aum stressed the potential salvation of all human beings. Asahara subsequently moved to Vajrayana Buddhism, which he came to believe predated Mahayana teachings. This step constituted a spiritual progression for Aum adherents to a higher religious state, limited to select practitioners. Aum's doctrinal interpretation of the earlier Buddhism, Reader thoughtfully writes, was that it "focused more specifically on the salvation of the individual and recognized that not all people were capable of gaining salvation."[53]

Asahara concludes *Supreme Initiation* with an apocalyptic vision of the world by predicting a catastrophic nuclear war provided that certain conditions were not fulfilled. The Japanese had attained a good life through hard work and sacrifice, but now a hedonistic life-style was destroying the nation. Economic decline would lead to an apocalyptic war against the United States which could only be averted if world leaders led their people to Asahara's brand of Buddhism.

Here Asahara's thinking parallels that of other apocalyptic movements: social criticism, a unique interpretation of the evolution of history, a prescription for the avoidance of disaster, and a distinct hope for world renewal through the teachings and practices of Aum. Robert Kisala notes critically:

> The salvation indicated here does not necessarily depend on mystic or spiritual agencies, but rather on the fact that the world can be convinced of the truth and follow a path of non-violence, led by Aum. Even if the predicted war cannot be avoided, however, the followers of Aum's practice will be protected, for they will be able to leave their bodies behind and enter into the Astral World...described as the Clear Light. Clearly this vision is still in its germinal stage. However, it does introduce one of the major themes elaborated on in later developments—the survival of those who have attained supernatural powers through Aum's practice.[54]

At this point in its development, Aum was dedicated to the optimistic pursuit of Mahayana's positivistic approach to the salvation of the world. Aum was vigorous in its advocacy of non-violence and universal Buddhahood which is realizable if we follow the ideal king of Shambala, who, of course, is none other than Asahara himself.

By 1990 Asahara started making increasingly pessimistic and fatalistic statements predicting the inevitability of world catastrophe and the ability of a small number of enlightened people to survive. Such thinking encouraged Aum to construct strong buildings where Aum faithful could retreat with the coming of inevitable nuclear war.

Asahara's view of Armageddon changed as he adopted his own version of Tibetan Buddhism. A catastrophic war was now inevitable and only the chosen few, those who had received superhuman power from Asahara himself, would survive to create a new world order.

The reason for his shift from Mahayana to his version of Vajrayana, however, is less clear. Asahara states that he was after an earlier and thus more authentic form of Buddhism. The transition period was also a time of stress for Aum. It was the time when it began its campaign of murder in 1989. Before 1989 Asahara described himself as a Buddhist prophet appointed by the Dalai Lama to restore authentic Mahayana Buddhism to Japan. By 1990, however, he began to view himself a *siddha* who was highly advanced in spiritual training and capable of supra-normal cognition and of marvelous feats such as levitation. The transition from a Mahayana to a Vajrayana approach marks more of a change in its prescription for a cure than in its diagnosis for the cause of human misery.

The Road to Armageddon: Aum Against the World

By the early 1990s Aum embarked on an intense campaign to arm itself. Eventually it developed facilities to produce deadly chemical gases such as sarin and was trying to build a supply of conventional weapons as well. It is as yet unclear whether Aum intended to use these weapons for self-defense against attacks from outside or whether it intended a series of violent attacks on society to create a state of instability that world war, Asahara's Armageddon, would inevitably occur.

During the early 1990s, Aum's growth as a terrorist group and its increasing acts of violence remained largely undetected. During this period Aum managed to build a worldwide organization and to accumulate a financial fortune, estimated at its peak to be above one billion dollars. It also developed and deployed, in Matsumoto, Tokyo and other locations, perhaps the most powerful arsenal of traditional and chemical weapons ever possessed and used by a terrorist group.

During the early and mid-1990s, Aum made extensive efforts in the United States, Russia and Australia to buy materials for nuclear and chemical weapons including highly sophisticated laser technology that the United States ordinarily refuses to sell to suspected terrorist countries. Aum was successful in purchasing some of the equipment that it sought, but most of the other attempts either fell through for a variety of reasons or were halted after the Tokyo subway gas attack. Nevertheless, Aum was able to develop a weapons arsenal in Japan unheard of in modern times.

Chapter IV
ᏸᎧᏑ
Aum's Appeal to Younger Japanese

A um became a haven for a few thousand younger Japanese—as well as a few middle-aged and elderly Japanese—who were either unable or unwilling to adjust to their highly conformist social environment. It appeared to the new members to offer a way out of the anomie of modern Japan.

Many Aum members apparently shared the misgivings that some young Japanese have with the current state of their society. They were born in the 1960s or early 1970s and have only known a prosperous Japan that was rapidly becoming one of the world's economic giants. Some of them were graduated from elite universities and could look forward to impressive careers in industry and government service. Other youthful members came from much less privileged backgrounds and were deeply frustrated over the unfavorable circumstances of their lives.

Since the late 1970s Japan, like many other modern industrial nations, has experienced a "religious boom" as many younger Japanese have joined a myriad of religious organizations and have sought ways to bring religion back into their lives. Increased concerns with the world's deteriorating environment and the problems of increased urbanization (including crime, difficulties in meeting career expectations, and family breakdown) have caused some younger and middle-aged Japanese to have greater doubts in the ability of Japan's postwar secular society to solve these problems. They are looking for alternative ideas to help them cope with these problems and often move their search to the mysterious and occult traditions of some religious belief systems to provide them with some solace.

The *shinshukyo* that grew in prominence after World War II through the 1970s satisfy a very different clientele than the *shinshinshukyo* of the late 1970s, 1980s, and 1990s. In other words, people who joined the Soka Gakkai, Rissho Koseikkai and Tenrikyo after World War II did so for very different reasons than the younger Japanese who joined Aum and other *shinshinshukyo* in great numbers a generation later.

The New Religions that grew in prominence in the 1950s and 1960s attracted great numbers of people who were not among the big winners of Japan's soaring economic growth of the early postwar era. As members of the lower-middle class, they held mundane poorly paid jobs at the lower spectrum of the service sector. They had also borne the brunt of the destruction of World War II and the immediate postwar era found them bankrupt both spiritually and materially. American authorities in the early stages of the Occupation (1945-52) had promised them a social revolution that focused on the rights and dignity of the average Japanese, but the "Reverse Course" during the latter half of the Occupation encouraged the formation of a new power elite in business, the bureaucracy and the political parties which paid little heed to the needs of ordinary citizens. Many "average Japanese" were victims of the "revolution of rising expectations" of the 1950s and 1960s. Their living standards did improve, but not as fast as the elite.

Many less advantaged Japanese joined the New Religions for a variety of reasons. The goals of most Japanese after the war were largely materialistic. The definition of success in life was a rapid rise in salary, a bigger and better home, and basic consumer goods. Some devotees of these new religions believed that their new faiths would bring them material success in life while others found solace with the company of new friends and a religious organization that ostensibly cared for them as people. Some of these religions also suggested that faithful devotees might find cures for psychological and physical ailments and published testimonies of members who described how their maladies had disappeared once they had adopted their new faiths. The frequent small-group-meeting formats of many of these religions provided a basic social life for previously lonely and isolated people.

The New Religions have a strongly "This Worldly" orientation where benefits are accrued in this lifetime. On occasion they may reject certain aspects of contemporary society and most acknowledge a belief in reincarnation, but they devote most of their time helping followers find a better life in the "here and now."

Contemporary Religiosity

Unlike previous periods, the present surge in religiosity is occurring in a society characterized by affluence and material security. For the most part it seems to be boredom with the routine and restrictions of the educational system and the business world that is giving birth to the new wave of seekers. Nishiyama suggests that many individuals see themselves as stuck on the escalator of modern bureaucratic society with little control or freedom to direct their own lives. For this reason, perhaps, magical religions which emphasize "sacred techniques for gaining power and well-being" are extremely attractive. While physical conditions have certainly improved since the war, a "new kind of poverty" has appeared and exists alongside material abundance. By-products of the modernization (rationalization) process have been boredom, fatigue, and the loss of meaning. Youth in particular, Nishiyama argues, have felt this new form of poverty most keenly as they are enclosed in a competitive and bureaucratic educational system from kindergarten to university.[1]

Frustrated by the world around them, some Japanese are turning to the frontier within their minds for greater freedom and happiness. This inner quest is part of the search of many youths for meaning in life. There is a reaction against traditional religion and culture. Many Japanese are turning to spirituality for the psychological assurances that material success has failed to provide.

Japan's Rebellious Youth

The younger generation of Japanese that came of age by the late 1970s, however, had a very different world view of their parents. They have grown up in an era of comparative affluence and total peace. While a vast majority of young Japanese continue to follow established paths of education and careers, a growing minority rejects various aspects of their parents' lives and seeks a more individualized and non-conformist life style. They belong to a new generation often labeled *shinjinrui* ("new human beings). According to Yukiko Tanaka:

> They are young men and women whose sensibility, taste, and philosophy are different from members of the generation that remembers childhood experiences of bombings and food shortages, who were single-mindedly involved in helping to make Japan the world's leading economic power.
>
> To many older Japanese, the term *shinjinrui* denotes decadence and a reaction against traditional values of diligence, discipline, and delayed gratification. *Shin-jinrui* are members of the generation who have grown up on new technology and a multitude of information sources, who consider work an unavoidable necessity, not a virtue. Instead of conformity, they value individuality, particularly in matters of personal taste...They are unwilling to sacrifice personal time for public causes and tend to be uninterested in participating in legitimate social and political protest.[2]

Two 1987 novels, *Noruue no Mori* (Norwegian Wood) by Murakami Haruki and *Kicchin* (Kitchen) by Yoshimoto Banana successfully portray members of this new generation. They are less conformist than their parents, are less willing to sacrifice their lives for any one corporation, and do not share their goals of material success. They are often loners with few connections to other people or, in fact, much of anything else around them. Their characters have a large number of casual relationships which in the long run prove to be rather shallow and unable to hide a prevailing sense of loneliness. Naoko, a young woman in *Noruue no Mori* who eventually kills herself after years of loneliness and deep depression, reflects back on her youth:

> The way I see it, we were living a borrowed existence, one we could never repay...We never paid our dues when we were supposed to ...We were naked babes playing on a deserted island. We got hungry, we ate bananas; we felt lonely, we slept together. It just couldn't last. We had to grow up and go out into society sometime.[3]

Murakami's main character, Watanabe Toru, is a college student living in a dormitory in Tokyo. He is a sensitive and warm person with good taste, but he lacks any real goal in life. He is in fact a loner unconnected with and uncommitted to the world around him. Watanabe reflects:

> The second week of September I arrived at the conclusion that my

so-called university education was absolutely meaningless. Still, I decided to perceive it all as an exercise in withstanding boredom. There was no compelling reason to quit school and go out into the world. There was nothing that I particularly wanted to do. So every day I went to the university, attended lectures, took notes, and in my free time read books and did research in the library.

Many younger Japanese today no longer share the materialistic drives of their parents. It is not hard to understand the appeal of a cult like Aum Shinrikyo, with its emphasis of Eastern mysticism as yoga, meditation, and Sanskrit mantras. Asahara, shrewdly sensing young people's needs, responded to their desire for self-improvement in a way that was clearly visible and easy to understand.He created a hierarchy that enabled members to rise in rank in accordance with their level of practice, the amount of money they donated, and other clear-cut gauges of contribution to the group.

Popular Culture

The Japanese media has detected to a New Age "religious boom" since the late 1970s that is associated in part with a recognition of the many problems of living in a rapidly changing modern society and the limitations of science in technology in resolving these problems in a post-industrial society. One finds many stories about the occult, mysticism, and the "spiritual world" in the media and in books and magazines. "New Age" magazines deal with such topics as UFOs, folk religion, divination, and channeling. There is also a "Science Fiction (SF) subculture" that found great appeal in such movies as "The Exorcist," "Poltergeist," the "Star Wars" trilogy, and the domestically-produced *Daireikai* [The great spirit world]. Popular science fiction animated movies like *Genma Taisen* and *Akira* popularized apocalyptic themes including the existence of a postapocalyptic community of superhumans, a theme found in the later publications of Aum Shinrikyo.[4]

There is also a major growth in interest in divination paralleling recent interest in astrology and fortune telling in the West. One finds palm readers in major public centers in Japanese cities such as Tokyo's Shinjuku Station who cater mainly to large groups of young educated office women who are eager to hear their fortunes. One may also see many women students on commuter trains poring over articles on divination in popular magazines that promise to tell the reader something about his future.[5] There is also an interest in new healing techniques and human potential courses that are often imported from the West.

There is only a tangential relationship between these themes of popular culture which are driven by the media and religious concerns. Comic-strip (*manga*) superhumans often have powers popularly associated with gods and demons. They sustain interest in nonrational or extrasensory topics, however, does have some genuine connections with modern religious trends in Japan.[6]

New Spirituality Movements in Japan

Shimazono uses the term "new spirituality movements" *(shin reisei undo)* that describe movements which are oriented towards a kind of loose community or network that are not formally structured as religions but which promote a world view or way of thinking that has religious elements. They often constitute an amorphous grouping of people with similar interests including the reading of the same books or participation in the same activities. However, they do not encourage the development of distinct religious doctrines or ritual and there is little emphasis on individual leadership as found in more formal religious organizations or movements.[7]

Shimazono describes five common characteristics of these movements:[8]

1. Stress is placed on a transformation of consciousness. Through the use of meditation or other, often psychological techniques a higher level of consciousness is sought, leading to the development of psychic powers or the ability to perceive mysterious phenomena.
2. A spiritual existence is believed to permeate the universe and be tangible to us on an intimate level. It is the deepening of the intercourse with this spiritual existence that is both the means and goal of the transformation of consciousness.
3. It is believed that a spiritual transformation of humanity is in the offing, and that the spiritual enlightenment of each individual contributes to this advancement.
4. It is further believed that individuals have within them-selves the power to arrive at this spiritual enlightenment, and that there is no need to rely on external powers or rituals. Traditional religion, which teaches such reliance, has only served to stifle the individual's enlightenment.
5. It is maintained that there is no opposition between religion and science, that the two are in fact one. However, there is a need to overcome the

false dualism found in modern science, which only serves to separate human beings from nature.

"New Spirituality Movements" in Japan sometimes exhibit pronounced apocalyptic thought that is connected with the recent popularization of Nostradamus' predictions of an impending world cataclysm.[9] These apocalyptic concerns, together with a concern for the transformation of consciousness and the impending start of a new spiritual age, contribute to the belief of some contemporary Japanese that the apocalypse can be avoided if enough people achieve transformation or that a postacolyptic group of supermen will survive the apocalypse and create a new world amidst the ruins of the old.[10] Aum Shinrikyo emphasized similar teachings in many of its publications after 1988.

Two Voices of the Aum Generation

The Kyoto-based NCC Study Center sponsored a 1995 seminar where several young people of the so-called "Aum generation" (people in their 20s and 30s) were invited to articulate their own perceptions about life in Japan with a focus on their own religious views and their reactions to the Aum affair.

Maeda Daisuke, a graduate of Doshisha University, remembers being alone much of the time before college. His parents, like so many others of their generation, were "irresponsible," abandoning their children to a life of loneliness while they pursued their part of the Japanese "miracle" of the 1960s and 1970s. Aum presented young people with an opportunity to find their own paths on their own while at the same time rejecting the "materialistic," yet meaningless lives of their parents.[11]

Miyai Rika, a doctoral student in Buddhist studies at Osaka University, at one time was attracted to Aum in her own search for religious practice and enlightenment. She depicts her interest in Aum (she never actually joined) against the background of the youth culture of the late 1980s and early 1990s. Her comments reflect much of what one reads about younger Japanese's sense of alienation.[12]

Firstly, concerning why, what was so attractive [about Aum], I think it was the idea of enlightenment (*satori*) and using one's own body in religious practices (*shugyo*). First, the established religions have merged into the everyday landscape....Because of this, it's very difficult for ordinary young people to join them. In addition, the new religions that arose after World War II...give the impression of being centered on this-worldly benefits, such as being healed from illness or freed from poverty. Our parents' and grandparents' generations, who were poor during and after the war, were I think looking during the post-war construction period for some sort of salvation they could see with their own eyes. At this time this-worldly benefits were very much emphasized. On the contrary, we of the so-called Aum generation didn't find this so attractive. Not this-worldly benefits, but enlightenment, deliverance (*gedatsu*), to receive spiritual salvation (*seishinteki ni sukuwareru*) were what we were earnestly seeking. And Aum placed enlightenment at the forefront, and furthermore one's own religious practice, to obtain enlightenment through religious practice using one's own body.[13]

Aum promised that anybody could achieve enlightenment based on one's own efforts and discipline, and that with this gain one could really change the world. There was also the idea that Japanese society—and the world as a whole—was heading towards inevitable collapse—increasing violence, pollution, global warming, etc. Her generation was also bombarded with television programs and cartoons depicting a final war between the forces of justice and evil invaders from outer space. Other people talked about Armageddon, but Aum's views received considerable publicity and were well-known among younger people. Even if most young people did not join Aum, the religion's teachings received considerable sympathy, especially when many youngsters, like Aum itself, felt rejected by and alienated from mainstream society.

Aum put forward the thesis that first came enlightenment or self-renewal, and that through spiritual change you would change the world. That appeared very attractive to me. They didn't emphasize Armageddon from the beginning, although they did use that word. If each one of us were to change spiritually, to become more spiritual, we could avert Armageddon, was the way they talked....

During the first half of the 1980s, when we were around high school age, there was a novel popular in some quarters by Hirai Kazumasa called *Genma Taisen* (*Great War With Deamons*); It later became an animated film [Armageddon], which communicated the same way of thinking. In other words, if we undertake spiritual training or religious practices, and attain a certain spiritual level, this world will in some way improve. The background to this was our consciousness of reality; I think that our generation has a very strong consciousness that this world is heading for destruction....For a long time I've felt deep anxiety that this is reality. However many slogans there are saying "Peace is good" or "Let's get rid of nuclear weapons," war hasn't ceased at all, nuclear weapons have not gone away, and I feel that these situations are pressing in....even though we would like to change politics for the better, in the past during the 1970s at the time of Ampo (The US-Japan Security Treaty) there may have been student violence and many conflicts, but actually it proved impossible to bring about any real change. So that illusion has been shattered and we do not know what to do....We suffer from the anxiety that however much effort we make, the world won't change, will it; it'll just continue on the path to destruction, won't it.

In addition, [the Japanese translation of] *the Prophesies of Nostradamus* came out in 1973, just when we were in elementary school, and through this the word "Armageddon" came into fashion. After that I and my friends unquestionably held the consciousness that soon Armageddon, the final war between good and evil, would take place. Against this background were television programs and *manga*; we might call to mind the Masked Rider (*kamen raidaa*) and *Ultraman*; in these, evil would invade the world, aliens or "shockers" or whatever, there was evil. Against these stood the Masked Rider or *Ultraman*, the upholder of justice, and that was us. Each of us would fight and destroy evil, justice would win; we had some sort of idea that we wanted to do something for the sake of justice. But when we grew up, we didn't know what justice might be, and evil in the world was not something tangible that we could see. Even if we say that politics is bad, assassinating the current prime minister is not going to change anything.

In that way, there was no longer anything to symbolize evil. So we did not know what to do with this sense of justice that had been cultivated within us. We felt extreme anxiety because we no longer knew what we should do, but we always had the feeling that something must be wrong. So through Armageddon surely something would end, evil would be destroyed, if Armageddon happened we would stand on the side of justice....But in reality it did not happen that way; we felt that more and more [the world] was heading in the direction of evil and destruction. In other words, I think that something like a hope for Armageddon....was building up inside us....

When you don't fit into the world's framework,...you feel some sort of sense of grievance or persecution...ordinary people bear it and go on with living. However, when Aum tried to set up various local groups, opposition movements took place...., and they were crushed. In addition, people sincerely left their homes (*shukke*)—leaving aside the question of whether that was a good thing or not—but their parents protested that they had been kidnapped or something. "Even though we are wholeheartedly acting for the sake of the truth, society does not accept us"—I think they must have felt this way very strongly. That when they (Aum members) reached that point, when they felt that they were being severely oppressed, and then when they heard that forcible investigations would start, then the idea of destroying the world arose, is of course something unacceptable and wrong, but I think I understand it a little. They were hoping for Armageddon. In other words, they wanted to destroy evil for the sake of justice, and they thought they wanted to make the world better; but as in reality we who have been wholeheartedly seeking truth are being persecuted by the world and regarded as evil, to put it another way, it is the society that is oppressing us that is evil, it is they who are in the wrong...So, why don't we destroy this mistaken world... shouldn't we rather than waiting bring about Armageddon ourselves, and if we do then the world of truth can be born. I do not think it is so strange that this kind of logic emerged.

The Otaku *Element of Japanese Society*

The term *"otaku* generation"[14] has gained currency in Japan during the 1990s to signify a growing number of young Japanese who reject communication with the outside world and withdraw into their own world where they consume themselves with computer video games and animated programs. Their lives differ markedly from the declining majority of mainstream young adults who follow traditional education and career paths and "street children" who are entirely caught up in the fads of the moment. *Otaku* youths have no set goals in life and have a tendency to remain in a world of dreams making do with a minimum of human relationships. It is apparent that most of Aum's youthful followers are from the *otaku* segment of Japanese society.

Non-*otaku* young adults characterize *"otaku*-people" as being very repressed sorts who remain alone in their apartments and rooms with their own videos and personal computers. They often dress in a non-conformist manner without any reference to current fashions or trends and limit their discussions with like-minded friends to computers and other related topics. They rarely date, refuse to work in career-oriented jobs or fields, and in every other sense resemble the stereotypical "computer nerds" of the West.[15]

Otaku youth spent much of their youth in the 1970s watching hours of cartoon shows based on various science fiction themes that often featured the idea of Armageddon. As early as 1976 my then-two-year-old daughter

Katie marveled at science-fiction like cartoons as *Uchusenkan Yamato* ("Spaceship Yamato") which dealt with young superheroes endowed with supernatural powers used to overcome powerful and evil enemies who seek to destroy the world.

The advent of the personal computer in the 1980s has led to the development of computer games and animated programs that deal with very similar themes which remain popular in the late 1990s. A highly celebrated animated television series of the mid-1990s, *Evangelion,* portrays a fourteen-year-old super-boy, Shinji Ikari, who fights to save a futuristic Tokyo by piloting his human-shaped robot, Eva, against mysterious evil enemies. *Evangelion,* however, is much more than just an action-thriller. The plot and sub-plots feature a series of riddles with strong psychological and religious themes. Shinji Ikari is a most reluctant hero who continually reflects on the evil nature of society, questions the necessity of remaining in a highly competitive and stressful world, and continually asks about the meaning of life.

Some Japanese sociologists speculate that the huge audience response for *Evangelion* among teenagers and young adults is because the show reflects the feelings and attitudes of millions of young Japanese today. These sociologists argue that *Evangelion* is a metaphor for the situation that these young Japanese find themselves in. Shinji Ikari was born in a world where his parents and their peers worked hard in stuffy companies and government offices. Their selfishness and immorality led them to virtually ignore their own children and brought acute suffering and violence to the world. Shinji Ikari inherits the putrefied world of his parents which he totally rejects.

The growing audience for *Evangelion* and books, games and fashions based on the show represent far more than just a fad. Sociologists wonder if the growing popularity of the show among more traditional young adults is a sign that they too are beginning to question the traditional Japanese values of "Work, honor and duty." Will the traditionalists become a minority in the near future? It is hard to say.

The late Ivan Morris, Professor of Japanese history at Columbia University, discussed the role of non-conformists in his classes and in his classic monograph, *The Nobility of Failure.* Using the analogy of Don Quixote attacking windmlls, Morris noted that Japan oftren has rebels, but can neither accept nor adapt to them. Japanese history is full of rebels who protested the norms of the establishment, but who ultimately were destroyed because there is no room for disharmony in a harmonious community. The failed rebel is often honored in Japanese society, but only after he is dead.

If one applies the same analogy to Aum, one might envision it as a self-proclaimed rebel group that stood in opposition to the norms of the establishment. Its anti-social stance and promises of sanctuary, enlightenment and superhuman powers appeared to be a haven for many dissatisfied youths. When Aum began to challenge society openly, its fate was sealed.

Chapter V
ഈറ
The True Believers of Aum

Although it has a healthy number of middle-aged and older members, Aum Shinrikyo is primarily a youth movement. The average age of the hard core member in 1995 was about 27 years. Young Japanese in their late twenties are facing one of the critical times of their lives. They are deciding whether or not to get married or whether to continue in a recent marriage. College-educated men and women have had a few years of corporate life and must decide whether an office job with all of its promises as well as tedium are what they really want.

The editors of *AERA*[1], a weekly news magazine published by *Asahi Shimbun*, did an in-depth study of thirteen young well-educated Aum members two months after the Tokyo gassing. They ranged in age from 23 to 38, came from highly successful families, and were all well-educated— 6 had graduated from Tokyo University, 3 from Waseda, and the rest from other highly regarded institutions. The people in this group were ordinary members of Aum, not the "elite" group of more established scientists and technicians (discussed later in this chapter) who formed Asahara's braintrust.[2]

AERA found that these young Aum members came from upwardly mobile families; although their parents had worked hard and followed traditional career paths to success, their children lacked the drive and motivation of their parents. They were generally quite withdrawn and anti-social while in middle school and high school. They had few if any real friends, were not interested in athletics, and rarely if ever participated in school-based clubs or other activities. They spent little time with their parents, who were too preoccupied with their own careers to pay much heed to their own children and families.

This group of young Aum members did well in primary and secondary school not because they were hard working students with clear educational goals, but, rather, because they were extremely bright and could do well with a minimum of effort. They spent their free time reading, playing with computers, and studying things of particular interest to them. They had no career goals, no clear political convictions and did not bother to vote or even pay any heed to election campaigns when they reached voting age, and never gave much thought about where they wanted to go to college.

These young adults took the entrance exams for Tokyo, Waseda and other universities not because they had any strong desire to attend these institutions and to use them as a base for successful careers. Rather, they complied with parental pressure to go to good schools and felt they had nothing better to do with their time. They were expected to go on to college and hoped to become independent within a college setting. If their parents were willing to pay their tuition and room and board, it was certainly better than staying at home doing nothing. They passed the entrance exams because of their native intelligence and because of information obtained through their own reading and experience.

College life is far easier for Japanese students than their counterparts in North America. Professors at Japanese universities where I have taught prepare interesting lectures but require far less daily work and are less strict in attendance policies than my colleagues in the United States. A college student even at an elite Japanese institution can survive by doing little work and only attending class on occasion.

The young Aum members rapidly found themselves quite bored with college life. They rejected the "economy-first" ethos of postwar Japanese life and looked, often desperately, for an alternative. Aum, brilliantly equipped with its blend of Eastern mysticism, yoga, and sanskrit mantras was like a proverbial powerful magnet. Quite often these susceptible youngsters met an Aum member, attended an on-campus lecture sponsored by Aum, or read an Aum publication that inspired them. They eventually joined Aum because they were looking for excitement, companionship, and were intrigued by the supernatural and "superman" ideas promoted by Aum. Their lack of any clear convictions or belief system allowed them to adopt Aum's ideology wholesale. As one of them told an *AERA* reporter, "We are children of a generation that has no personality." Aum gave them identity.[3]

One would have thought that the entire movement would have collapsed immediately after the sarin incident, but many members stayed on for weeks and months. One determined believer, Fuji Noatsushi, a 34-year-old two-year member from Fukui said in June 1995 that Aum had become the pillar of his life, that he believed deeply in Aum's teachings, and that, frankly speaking, he had nowhere else to go. He had joined with a number of other people from Fukui, and although some members of this group had left the religion, he and a few others were determined to stay on.[4] Other members simply hung on because they had donated all of their possessions to Aum and simply had no other place to go.[5]

The Tokyo Broadcasting System broadcast a program on 19 July 1995 reporting the results of a survey of former Aum members who had later apostatized. They announced that the most appealing aspects of Aum to the former members were its austere religious practices, the promise that true believers could be somehow delivered from this-worldly attachments, the many paranormal psychological experiences professed by Asahara and his top associates, and the promise that they could join a community of similarly motivated peers. An additional factor especially appealing to older inductees was the promise of spiritual healing.[6] Famed Japanese novelist Murakami Haruki has built a reputation as a novelist who depicts the alienation of Japanese youth, but after the Aum incident he temporarily moved away from fiction to interview and write about the victims of Aum—people personally injured by Aum violence as well as the ordinary members of Aum who joined the sect to escape from the misery or boredom of their own lives but who played no role in Aum's campaign of terror. Murakami's 1997 book *Andaaguraundo* (Underground)[7] describes the long-term suffering of many of the victims of the subway sarin attack.

Murakami analyzed what he had learned about Aum members in a brief May 1998 article in the *Yomiuri Shimbun*.[8] Murakami brilliantly diagnoses the worldview and concerns of Aum youth in this piece:

> Aum Shinrikyo can be considered the ultimate of "social abnormality," but as far as I can see, it was born of extraordinary "ordinariness...." If we look at the eight people I have interviewed so far, they all seem ordinary on the surface. They were all brought up in ordinary homes and had money. All of the men were popular with women. But they would tell me, "even though we were in extremely good shape, we felt as if there was a gaping hole in our bodies; our hearts were cold."
>
> I understand their motives to some extent—they could not cope with

society's values and decided to join the spiritual world. It reminded me of my own generation's student movement in the 1960s. The movement was a way of saying "no" to Japan as it existed during that period of high economic growth.

The cult members were also saying "no" to bubble-economy Japan and its superficiality. (Saying "no") is not at all a bad thing. Although what guru Shoko Asahara did angers me, we just can't dismiss the reasons people joined Aum.

In our time, there was a political way out. When Tokyo University student Michiko Kanba died in 1960 during the student protest of Japan's signing of the US-Japan security treaty, we knew that we would have another chance in 1970, when the renewal of the treaty was to be debated. In other words, we knew where we stood.

However, young people these days feel that political action is useless. So they come to these sudden decisions to seek a spiritual solution....(The Aum disaster) is not solely their own faults as individuals. The evil of an individual is partly a reflection of the evil of the system (that produces him or her). The sarin attack was a product of the evil of Asahara, but this evil is related to the evils of our society: the ambiguity of the system; the lack of freedom of information; people uncritically following what the authorities tell them to do. We just can't decry Asahara's evil and ignore the rest of society.

The Great Hanshin Earthquake and the sarin attack were highly symbolic, related incidents. The two may look like random events, but if the earthquake had not revealed certain problems within our postwar society, such as engineers doing a poor job of constructing buildings, the sarin attack might not have happened.

Evil exists in every age and I, too, come across it in my own life. But society should be able to absorb it, within certain bounds. Present-day Japan, however, does not have this ability. There is no effective, normal, subsocial system that can absorb people who cannot function in mainstream society.

Popular Culture as a Means of Recruiting Youths

Aum leaders shrewdly recognized the potential for membership growth if it could attract swarms of young members. Aum made every effort to attract the attention of many younger Japanese through a sophisticated public relations campaign that included the publication of many *manga* magazines and several animated films.

Manga are extremely popular in Japan[9], reaching over two-thirds of the nation's senior high school students. The potential of *manga* as a method of influencing the thinking of Japanese youth has long been recognized by the Japanese media. Millions of young Japanese also frequently watch animated cartoons (*anime*) on television. The themes or story-lines of *manga* or *anime* deal with science fiction. Popular programs like *Uchu Senkan Yamato* (Space Battleship Yamato) and *Mirai Shonen Konan* (Conan, Future Boy) have entertained younger Japanese for many years.

Frederik L. Schodt, an American student of Japanese *manga*, was impressed with Aum's sophisticated use of *manga* to proselytize its views:

> One secret of the cult's success...was its ability to package its twisted message in an attractive fashion.... Anime and manga—because they are so popular, because they can be used to dramatize and exaggerate information and simplify a complex reality—were the perfect vehicle for the cult to proselytize.[10]

One of the last issues of *Aum Comic*[11] contains four cartoon version stories by Aum artist-writers about the experiences of younger people who had joined the group. Before encountering Aum they had been adrift in a life without meaning, but how they had found happiness, peace, and, in one case, superhuman strength. There is the clear message that Asahara had a humble start in life, but through hard work and visits with spiritual leaders in India he had the power to save others and help them survive the forthcoming Armageddon. Each story implies that anyone who follows Asahara's teachings can acquire his powers without fail. The comics also contain brief articles featuring messages and instruction by Asahara as well as a whole host of advertisements for various Aum products including telephone cards bearing pictures of some Aum leaders as well as advertisements for Aum books, restaurants, and public lectures.

Aum also produced *Spirit Jump*, a three-volume set of paperback books consisting of cartoon-style stories of various disciples who had "become disillusioned with their humdrum, spiritually empty lives in modern Japan, joined the cult and found happiness." The stories are rendered in a variety of styles, including the typical *shojo* (girls') style complete with bug-eyed cute characters and flowers to highlight emotions and sensitivity.[12] These books are identical in length, style, and quality to mainstream *manga* books and were sold in mainstream chain bookstores.

Although there is little published evidence that Aum's *manga* publications brought many new members into the organization, they must have had some effect and made some money, because Asahara maintained his own in-house staff to prepare a variety of publications over a period of several years. Since Aum used *manga* and *anime* as key proselytizing tools, it is possible that some young members first heard or became attracted to Aum by reading its popular culture publications.Asahara was himself a big fan of *manga* and animation when he was a child—as a child he is said to have dreamed of one day building a "robot empire"—and many Aum *manga* resemble popular *manga* themes and story-lines.[13]

Asahara also made use of animated films to advertise the benefits of Aum membership. Asahara's personality and his supposed supernatural powers were very attractive to a number of younger members. Asahara frequently told audiences that he had acquired six mystic powers in Tibet after punishing training. These supposed powers enabled him to levitate, to transform himself into any form, and to move objects and to change their forms without touching them.

Asahara's supposed supernatural abilities were shrewdly advertised in Aum's extensive and very slickly polished promotional material. One animated film, for example, showed a handsome and lean Asahara —quite a contrast from his homely and stout demeanor —going through walls and serenely flying over cities[14], bringing to mind perhaps Muhammad's legendary flight to Jerusalem from Mecca. One would think that a sophisticated people like the Japanese would laugh loud and long at such propaganda, but Asahara's supposed supernatural powers rank high on the list of why people joined Aum.

Aum Shinrikyo also very cleverly sought to enhance its legitimacy by showing pictures in its publications of Asahara meeting and supposedly receiving the endorsements of major Buddhist and Hindu clerics. One glossy booklet depicting Asahara's spiritual career handed to this writer on a Kyoto street corner in May, 1995 has a picture of a splendidly attired Asahara on the cover and a headline in Japanese reading, "The True Path of Salvation through Tibetan Buddhism."[15] Lengthy articles with accompanying pictures describe Asahara's contact with many of the leading figures of Tibetan Buddhism including Khamtul Rinpoche, Kalu Rimpoche, and the Dalai Lama. Asahara's meeting with the Dalai Lama is described in detail.Asahara claims that the latter not only instructed him in some of the deeper aspects of Buddhism, but also admonished him to spread the true Buddhism to Japan.

Asahara's highly chronicled meetings with these highly respected Tibetan leaders gave him an aura of respectability with some members and intellectuals and journalists that he might not otherwise have had. Shinichi

Nakazawa, a professor of religion at Chuo University supports this view, adding that when he first met Asahara in 1989, he found him to be both humorous and rational, while at the same time unsophisticated and unrestrained, traits that most Japanese have lost. Hiromi Shimada, a former professor of religion at Japan Women's University, also had a favorable impression of Asahara after meeting him in 1990:

> Asahara did not seem like a cult leader because he was frank and had a good knowledge of things like cars and professional baseball. He appeared to be a commonplace, amicable person who liked to sing although he could not sing well. But I got the impression that he was extremely smart. People with an impressive academic background became followers because they sensed his intelligence.[16]

Aum's Older Members

Although Aum was and still is primarily a "youth" movement, one cannot ignore the fact that it had a noticeable minority of middle-aged and elderly members as well. When Asahara left Agonshu and formed Aum in the mid-1980s, a handful of Agonshu faithful in their 30s and 40s came with him. Testimonials in early Aum publications (1987-89) include pieces by many older members. Only in the early 1990s did Aum take on a far more youthful look.

Aum's older members are mainly female—housewives in their late thirties to early fifties who have suffered from a combination of physical ailments and mental depression. In this sense Aum resembles several of the larger *shinshukyo* of the 1960s and 1970s— such as the Soka Gakkai— who also attracted a large number of middle-aged female members. There is a much more even distribution of men and women joining Aum after 1990 than in the 1980s.

Older members had different reasons for joining Aum than their younger counterparts. Their major concerns were physical—one complained of a bad ulcer, another of severe headaches and acute weight loss, while others complained of the normal "aches and pains" of the aging and aged. Some older members confess that their failures and disappointments in life had led to severe abuses of alcohol or drugs. They all claim that Aum's therapeutic treatments cured them of their ailments and allowed them to live healthy and active lives.

The members of other *shinshukyo* in the 1960s and 1970s also joined because of the promise of a physical cure. Soka Gakkai testimonials are full of tales of people who were ill or in pain, but who achieved a miraculous cure after they chanted the Gakkai's mantra before its object of worship. Today Soka Gakkai testimonials have moved away from physical to such psychological problems as severe depression and loneliness. One also finds this trend in Aum testimonials.

Aum's Scientific Elite

Yamaori Tetsuo, a scholar with a long professional interest in Aum, states that there are three groups of people within Aum. "At the top are the leaders—Asahara's closest advisors and friends; next come the upper level authorities who are extremely knowledgeable about science and highly skilled in the use of advanced technology and information equipment; below them are the true believers who have taken the tonsure and abandoned normal life to seek salvation in their master."[17]

The scientists, engineers and technicians who helped form Asahara's "brain trust" were distinctly older than the average recruit. They ranged in age from their late twenties to early forties and generally were in the early stages of their careers.

Aum Shinrikyo did not simply wait for potential members to show up at its meetings. It actively proselytized a number of talented graduate students in the hard sciences, luring them with promises of unlimited research funds, state-of-the-art laboratories and other inducements. Since their most likely alternative was a career in the regimented laboratories of large corporations with no opportunities to conduct their own research and writing, Aum's offer was quite attractive. Aum also successfully pursued a few members of Japan's Self-Defense Forces who had skills in weaponry and modern military technology.

It is hard to determine the true feelings and intentions of Aum's leaders. Were they religious leaders on a crusade for happiness and compassion? Were they con artists and criminals who stole from followers for their own enrichment and lust for power? Tetsuo suggests that Asahara and his braintrust were not the devout religious people they claimed to be. Rather,

Aum's leaders considered themselves elite intellectuals, revolutionaries dissatisfied with the stuffy stable world they saw around them. They were political technocrats, tired of a fat, lukewarm society. Possessed of hypertrophied imaginations, they were convinced they could change people and build a perfect state.[18]

Sociologists have also tried to speculate as to why a number of young intellectuals joined Aum in the early 1990s and then joined in a violent crime wave a few years later. One big attraction was the fact that while working in the "real" world, they were no more than small cogs in big wheels, but in the secluded world of Aum, one could become, for example, chief of the cult's science and technology agency and do whatever one wanted at an impressive facility with a great deal of money.

It is also important to note that while these intellectuals graduated from some of the better schools in Japan, they were rarely at the top of their classes. They were good students, but not quite good enough to be at the cutting edge, to be among the tiny few who would make the fast-track to the tops of their fields. This can be very frustrating for a bright person who has come so close to making it to the very top, yet just missed it. Aum seemed to offer these people a second-chance at a shining career.

Aum offered scientists and engineers, who had little chance to exhibit their creativity working for larger companies, the unheard of chance to experiment and do research in an open environment with highly modern equipment and no restrictions on how they worked. Winston Davis suggests that "one reason some technicians and engineers joined Aum was to accelerate their own scientific careers. The Millennium Kingdom offered talented young people instant recognition. Why spend years in Tokyo's meritocratic rat race, when overnight you can become a mover-and-shaker in Aum's Construction, Intelligence, or Health and Welfare Ministry."[19]

Dr. Hayashi Ikuo, a well-educated heart surgeon, actively participated in the sarin poisoning in March 1995 and received a sentence of life imprisonment in late May 1998. Although he was older than most of Asahara's braintrust, his story, portrayed here in the *Yomiuri Shimbun*[20], is not untypical of other intellectuals "seduced" by Aum:

> Watching a remorseful Dr. Ikuo Hayashi weep and wail in the court room, many in the gallery could not help but wonder how this former elite heart surgeon became involved in a chain of crimes unprecedented in postwar Japan, leading to his being sentenced to life in prison Tuesday.
>
> Having worked at a Detroit hospital and then as head of a national hospital in Ibaraki Prefecture, Hayashi began to search for what he thought modern science lacked. He found his answer in Buddhism. Hayashi joined

the Agonshu religious cult before meeting Shoko Asahara and joining Aum Shinrikyo in 1989.

The following year, he became a resident follower at the cult's compound in Yamanashi Prefecture, bringing with him his wife, also a medical doctor, and two children. At the time, the primarily pure hearted Hayashi never doubted that Asahara was a Buddhist emancipator with supernatural power.

Hayashi remained faithful to Asahara. However, Asahara didn't like him very much, Hayashi said. "(Asahara) was always distant to me," Hayashi told a court hearing. "Maybe he was feeling a sense of inferiority for what I once had—a good family, education and profession. My presence was something that reminded him of his past frustrations."....

After joining the cult, Hayashi gradually began to see its dark side—narcotics, guns, kidnapping and the murder of dissidents. But he could not oppose Asahara's orders because of his blind belief in the cult's leader and the fear that he, too, might be killed if he defied him, he told the court.

He has described in court the three levels of experience feared by followers if they opposed Asahara's orders. "The first level is that you are ignored by Asahara and you are denied religious training...At the second level, you are told that you will go to hell if you betray him. Finally, you get involved in a homicide and realize that the next victim could be you."

As Hayashi's need for Asahara's care and attention grew, his ethics as a doctor began to fade. He started applying his professional knowledge to the cult's criminal acts. Hayashi invented "narco," an interrogation method using the anesthetic thiopental sodium, and "new narco," a method of erasing unpleasant memories of the cult from a follower's brain by using electrical shocks and narcotics.

He also helped produce LSD, which was mixed into drinks used during initiation ceremonies. When Asahara made the followers drink them, the drugs caused hallucinations, leading initiates to believe that they were witnessing the power given off by Asahara.

During his transformation from a doctor into a defendant accused of multiple murders, Haysashi said he gave up one thing—the ability to think for himself. "Everybody called Asahara 'guru.' We left all judgement to Asahara. When Asahara called it salvation, everything was justified, even murder." Hayashi told the court.

Since his arrest, which came a month after the March 1995 gas attack, Hayashi seems to have returned to reality. He renounced his loyalty to Asahara, confessed his illegal acts and motivated other accused cultists to tell the truth in court. Most of all, he has shown repentance for his crimes. "The two died because they bravely picked up the plastic bags (of sarin) in an attempt to restart subway operations," Hayashi said at a December 11 court hearing, referring to the subway workers killed by the sarin he

released. "And I, as a doctor, was supposed to save people's lives, but..,"
he broke off.

Dr. Hayashi and many of the other well-educated leaders of Aum are
also victims. Although he is today a convicted murderer, there is no real
indication that he began his career in a criminal fashion. They joined Aum
probably anticipating a path to a better life, but they soon found themselves
drawn into a cataclysm of crime that proved hard to escape.

The Earnestness of Aum Members and the Question of Brainwashing

The recent "cult" tragedies involving such groups as the People's Temple
(Jonestown), the Branch Davidians, the Solar Temple, Heaven's Gate as
well as Aum Shinrikyo have given "cults" and newly founded religions and
religious groups a very bad name.

Newspapers and popular magazines have told bizarre stories about life
in such groups, often depicting "cult" members as mindless zombies. We
often hear lurid tales relating how innocent individuals are trapped in cults
through sleep deprivation, protein-deficient diets, and extreme isolation from
family and friends. Such tales create the strong impression that people join
new religious movements mainly because their leaders are in some
mysterious way able to "control" the minds of their converts. This control
is often called "brainwashing" and is associated with "psychological
manipulation and emotional blackmail."[21]

Watanabe Manabu, a member of the Nanzan Institute for Religion and
Culture, writes that Japan has experienced considerable anti-cult hysteria as
a result of the Aum incident.[22] Anti-cult journalists and other spokesmen
appeared on endless television talk shows preaching the line that although a
small number of executive members of Aum were guilty of horrible deeds,
the average Aum members were sincere and innocent people who should
receive public sympathy and support in their efforts to readapt to ordinary
society. The implication was that Asahara and his top lieutenants had engaged
in a form of brainwashing whose purpose was intended to "force somebody's
ideology, assertions, and thinking to change drastically."[23] The Tokyo District
Prosecutor's Office apparently accepted this line of reasoning, stating that
the sarin incident on the Tokyo subways was carried out by Aum as a highly
closed group, and that prosecution of some participants might be difficult

because some members were under "mind control."[24]

Watanabe, who has interviewed a few former Aum members at length, feels that the mindset of the communal member is too complex to simply explain as "mind control." Watanabe notes that the former Aum members he met all joined Aum through their own free will. "They were hoping to achieve their own spiritual development and were attracted to Aum for a variety of reasons. Nobody forced them to join or to remain at the centers."[25]

Once they joined and lived in an Aum commune, however, life became more complicated and it was not easy to leave. It is well-documented that Aum leaders made every effort to keep members from defecting. Aum's first murder in February 1989 was a young man who tried to defect[26] and there are accounts of Aum officials chasing after defectors and bringing them back by force. It is also true that members quite often were deprived of sleep, confined alone in small cubicles for many hours while being forced to listen to Asahara's sermons or Aum-inspired music. There are also accounts of members who were fed drinks laced with LSD or other drugs.

Press reports of Aum followers often give the strong impression that they were brain-washed sickly drugged robots who blindly followed the "Guru's" every whim. That may have been the case for a few members in the mid-1990s, but scholars who visited Aum meetings before 1994 report a very different story. They often saw excited people who felt that they had found real meaning in life, a real answer to their problems. Richard Young, a scholar of Japanese religion, attended an Aum meeting in 1990 in Yokohama at the invitation of a young Aum member, "Nagasena" (not his real name) who resembles the thirteen members discussed in *AERA*. Young found a meeting hall located in a shabby part of the city and had none of the fancy glitter or cleanliness of the offices and community centers of other new religious groups. There was nothing extraordinary about the meeting except the lively excited atmosphere which gave the place an "allure that was riveting."[27]

He found the Aum members there, including a middle-aged company employee, an "elderly matron distributing home-baked cookies, and a bevy of young girls emblazoned with Mickey and Daffy," to be to engrossed in their studies of Asahara's writings to pay much attention to a foreign guest. There was something electric going on—Asahara is a charismatic speaker who can inspire and amuse those in his presence. It was one thing to read Asahara's words in his books and another to hear him speak in person.

If you had been there, I think he might have almost convinced you that the Buddha was alive again and that the possibility of you becoming a Buddha too, might not be so remote. What originally sparkled with wit, humor and flashes of insight became flat, pedantic and redundant when confined in print....[28]

Young left the Yokohama Aum center with no deep fears that Aum was the dangerous group being portrayed by some media writers.

Indeed, I convinced myself that there might even be a certain value in its enforcement of a tough Buddhist regimen, unlike the coddling, feel-good-about-the-ancestors-but to hell-with-the-precepts attitude of the established Buddhism I was familiar with. There was moreover not holy nostrum, magical potion, chant or all-purpose amulet the Master was purveying upon the witless public that I was aware of, but only yogic hardship and ascetic agony....[29]

Young, the serious scholar who never seriously considered joining Aum or any other New Religion, initially found in Aum what many educated Japanese saw who actually joined Aum or sympathized with its teachings and motives:

Behind all the Aum bashing by the media and the plaintive wails of distraught parents, I thought I could detect a pattern of objections to the renunciatory form of Buddhism that matched what had been heard all over East Asia, not only Japan, since the era of its introduction into this region. Whenever the world and its ways have been rejected and a separate community of renunciates has been established, Buddhism—or whatever goes by that name —has been denounced as economically unproductive and the Buddhist monks who have been sexually unreproductive have been traduced as unfilial. Productivity and reproductivity are the essential ingredients of the pervasive *musubi* (growth) one finds in Japan. Aum was obviously a threat to both.[30]

It is clear that most members who joined Aum did so of their own free will and that they willingly remained as members. Despite the horror stories published in the popular press in the days and weeks after the 1995 sarin gas attack, many if not most members were content with their lives and had no desire to rejoin life in the "real world."

Chapter VI

ଚ୨ଔଃ

The Voices of Aum

Many journalists, scholars, psychologists and other professionals have analyzed various aspects of the Aum phenomenon, but there is perhaps no better way to begin to understand a movement than through the words and thoughts of its members. This chapter presents an overview of Aum members through a collection of testimonials by Aum faithful and interviews with a variety of scholars and journalists.

There are four identifiable categories of Aum members. First, there are very "ordinary" young members. They consist of high school graduates and college "dropouts" who were either unemployed or employed in low-skill service or factory jobs.The second group consists of college students or recent college graduates who for a variety of reasons had opted not to seek a mainstream career and way of life. The third category includes highly trained professionals dissatisfied with their careers. The fourth group consists of a small group of older members, often housewives and older women, who lack professional skills and who have led quiet lives.

Category I: Ordinary People

Scholars and journalists who interviewed Aum members following the Tokyo sarin gas incident focused on younger well-educated members. They tended to ignore a significant grouping of more "ordinary" less-educated members who had been "drifting" through life without any significant sense of direction. These members, often in their twenties, were in many cases only average high school students who participated in few if any activities, lacked the ambition to prepare for and take the rigorous entrance college entrance exams, and had few close friends.Acquaintances often criticized their "passive" approach to life.Many of them worked as store clerks, waiters, or in garages or small factories where they obtained very low salaries.

Celebrated novelist Murakami Haruki is one of the few Japanese writers to interview these "ordinary" Aum followers. One of Murakami's most telling pieces provides the biography of Kanda Miyuki, a young woman born in 1973 who joined Aum when she was sixteen years old.[1]

Case 1: Kanda Miyuki

Kanda Miyuki's (henceforth KM) life was very normal. She grew up in a thoroughly middle-class family in Kanagawa Prefecture with her parents and two older brothers. Her father is an average "salaryman" who spent long hours at his office each week, but who took his family on frequent outings on Sundays. KM remembers him as a strict disciplinarian in stark contrast to her mother who was always gentle *(yasashii)* and caring. KM remembers that her parents always stressed the importance of education as a means of getting ahead in life.

KM never indulged much in club or social activities in high school. She had a number of casual acquaintances, but nobody who could be considered a "best friend." She enjoyed spending her free time at home alone, reading novels (mainly science fiction) and watching animated programs on television. KM was an average student. She did her homework in a careless manner and quite often lapsed into daydreams while in class. KM had no plans or ambitions about the future despite the fact that her parents were always encouraging her to work hard.

KM relates that she lived in a very active dream world. Her dreams seemed too real to her—she dreamt that she could soar through the air, that she had gained superhuman strengths. She frequently mixed her dream world and the real world in her memory and imagination. When KM was sixteen, her two older brothers gave her several Aum books and pamphlets that had caught her attention. Asahara's book *Supreme Initiation* especially interested her. Here she first heard of Asahara's alleged sacred powers, including levitation, and his promise to bestow these powers on his most faithful followers. KM hoped to realize these powers, including the ability to fly, which she had heretofore only experienced in her dreams.

> KM and her two brothers decided to join Aum in 1989 at its Setagaya (Tokyo) branch office. At first their participation was quite minimal. They each paid a nominal 30,000 yen (about $325) admission fee and attended yoga classes at an Aum center in the Tokyo area. At first her parents voiced little objection because they thought that Aum was little more than a yoga club that might actually benefit their children.

KM found friendship and a real sense of direction in Aum, so much so that she decided to become a full-time member of the Aum community (*shukke*) along with her two brothers. Her parents tried to persuade her against making such a rash move, but she and her brothers left home entirely, quit school, and became dedicated disciples of Asahara himself.

KM initially lived in the Aum compound in Yamanashi prefecture near Tokyo and then bounced between Aum quarters in Setagaya and elsewhere. She spent a considerable amount of time meditating, but she also worked very hard as a cook and a desk clerk. Life was not easy, but it seemed fulfilling. There was a sense of purpose—Aum was to lead the world to a higher realm of understanding, and peace and by participating as a full-time member of Aum, KM was making her own contributions to world peace.

KM was at the Aum compound in Kamikuishiki on 20 March 1995 when she heard the TV news of the sarin attack. She was stunned and incredulous over reports that Asahara and other Aum leaders had both planned and carried out the attack. Surely the reporters were mistaken? Was it not in reality an attack staged by the government or some other religious organization to throw the blame on Aum?

KM stayed in the Aum compound even when it was raided by police. She had devoted every moment of her life to Aum for over six years. She firmly believed in the power and divine guidance of Asahara. KM also realized that she had no place to go. Thus, even during the most difficult days during the summer of 1995, she stayed on with Aum and was an active member as of summer 1998.

What is striking about KM is indeed her "extraordinary ordinariness." She lacked the education or personal wealth of other Aum members mentioned in the previous chapter, but she shared their loneliness, absence of ambition, closeness to their families, and general lethargy. She was not a genuine "otaku," but she shared their traits, especially their sense of alienation. Aum gave her a sense of belonging, participation and purpose she had never experienced before.

Case 2: Akimoto Seiko

Akimoto Seiko was a twenty-four-year-old store clerk in Hokkaido when she joined Aum in December 1988. She was living with her parents, was unmarried, had few friends, and had no clear direction in life.She presents her story in a "Testimony" published in the September 1989 issue of the *Mahayana News Letter.*

I joined Aum last December (1988) influenced by the manager of the shop where I work. I had no idea what I was getting myself, into, initially hated the practice, and was not very active. Then that horrible winter came again and I experienced terrible frostbite on my foot. It became itchy, turned red and swollen, and the skin cracked open in parts. Medicine helped for a while, but could not get rid of the condition.

Aum forbade the use of medicine. I decided to cease taking medicine orally and only bound my feet with a bandage and ointment. But then the frostbite got continually worse. Seeing my tormented condition, Master Asahara answered: "The cause of the frostbite is the weakened Apana (one of the vital energies of the body); the practice of Sukha Purvaka Pranayama should cure it." My practice began.I began to practice at home, but had to do secretly because my family hated religions. It took a lot of courage to do it at home.

One night when I was practicing in the living room, my father woke up to go to the bathroom. He noticed the light and peeked in. He said, "What in the world are you doing? Go to bed now!" I explained, "This is how I cure my frostbite. Don't worry. I won't be late for work tomorrow." My mother, who learned of the incident from my father, asked me, "Please don't do anything funny at home."

It didn't take long until my mother discovered that I had joined Aum. She gasped, "Don't tell me that you are doing the same thing as the shop manager." But when I told her the truth, she only mumbled, "Oh Dear!" But I got worried a few days later when she said, "I'm about to have a nervous breakdown." But an Aum leader at the Aum center said, "No matter what happens, continue your practice." I obeyed him. I just ignored all of the ugly things my family said about Aum—I just wished they would understand.

As my practice improved, my icy feet began to show some improvement. The itchiness and swelling were gone and the skin started to peel off. After two weeks I no longer needed the ointment or bandage. I could not believe it. It was a big "Wow!" The frostbite condition that had afflicted me for 20 years was no longer a source of pain or worry.

When I told my mother about it, she said, "Oh dear, but its been rather warm this winter" and father made even more sarcastic remarks about Aum. But I know better. It happened because I believed in Master Asahara and practiced what he said faithfully. You should all believe in Master Asahara; then you'll have nothing to fear.

Case 3: Uda Kazuhisa

Uda Kazuhisa was a 20-year-old part-time worker in Saitama Prefecture near Tokyo when he submitted the following testimony to the October 1991 Aum *Mahayana News Letter.*

I first knew Master Asahara and Aum in the article concerning air-levitation in *MU* magazine (1985). Though I had a strong impression, I did not have a desire to enter Aum then. Later, I read the Secret Development of Supernatural Powers and had a strong shock. Because I was deeply interested in things mystical and had a desire to actually practice since junior high school, Aum held a special fascination for me.

Since I had felt that independent practice was both difficult and dangerous, I wished to practice under a Guru to awaken my Kundalini quickly and safely. When I read a book by Asahara, I contacted the seminary and asked to just look on. They did not accept me as a spectator, but sent me a guide for Aum's concentrated seminar including a leaflet and Aum's book, *Beyond Life and Death.* I read the book and at once knew that Master Asahara had attained the final enlightenment and become a Buddha.

At the seminar, I had Shaktipat and really felt the existence of Kundalini. I entered Aum in January, 1987. Later I had some mystical experiences including a vision of light during meditation, Nada sound, and the separation of the Lower Astral Body. These experiences deepened my faith as I knew them previously in the teachings of Aum. Mentally, I had difficulties several times, but they could be got over through the advice of the and other leaders, and I was able to look at myself more coolly than before.

As to the experience during Initiations other than Shaktipat, the changes I had after "Initiation of Love," which was performed during the Guru Yoga Initiation at the beginning of last year (1990), were really remarkable. As soon as I drank the Master's DNA (blood, ed.), my whole body became hot and remained hot for several hours. As I had not experienced such strong heat before, I was really surprised at the effect of this Initiation.

My dream to be a disciple of a Buddha like Shakyamuni has come true. Also, enlightenment was a mere dream for me before I entered Aum, but now the door is open. I hope that you can find the true Way which is superior to the mundane world which is full of temporary enjoyments.

Uda's experience reminds one of KM. He lacks the education of some of the other members, and he does not seem terribly alienated from society. But, like so many other Aum members, his life was excruciatingly ordinary, and he convinced himself that Aum provided him with something extraordinary.

Category Two: The Alienated Students

Many of Aum's youthful members were college dropouts or recent graduates. They refused to enter the mainstream corporate realm of their parents and instead sought a world that would have greater meaning and companionship for them. They felt marginalized socially and sought a new community willing to accept them. An Aum member told a journalist:

> All the people at Aum were always cheerful and never said bad things about others, which was quite unlike ordinary society! I could see that it was actually brighter than the other places outside. Here we see the creation of a new community at the margins of society that is to become the ideal Buddhist land Shambhala.

A doctoral student who left a good job at a major trading company confessed: "I had enough of the materialistic world of business. I could not figure out what I should do or why I was there. " When he attempted the meditation techniques advocated by Aum, he exclaimed: "I felt this bursting sensation from inside. It was amazing.! I felt as if I had ascended to a higher stage. A bright light fell from above and entered me."[2]

Maki Taro, a former editor of the magazine *Sunday Mainichi* and an early critic of Aum notes:

> In a country whose fathers are utterly preoccupied with work, whose mothers want their children to be winners and whose educational system prides itself on the fiercest of competition for admission, these new-new religions… are attractive to kids who don't make the cut, or those who do but see little purpose in their lives. [3]

The following cases introduce a number of college students, graduates and dropouts who say they found relevancy and meaning in life once they joined Aum.

Case 1: The Tragedy of Nagasena

A knowledgeable scholar of Japanese religions, Richard Young, penned one of the best accounts of an alienated Aum member.The following passage is useful not only for its depiction of a follower of Asahara, but also for Young's analysis of Aum's appeal to surprisingly large segment of Japan's younger citizens.Young described the life of a former student Nagasena (introduced in the previous chapter) whom he first met in 1990 shortly after Aum's election debacle. Young remembers the period when he first met Nagasena:[4]

> Back then.... Aum was barely a ripple upon a placid surface of my liberal academic consciousness. There was more publishable research to be done on Japanese new religions other than Aum.... Had it not been for Nagasena, I would have been culpably ignorant, for a person in my profession, of why a not insignificant number of young people (as well as a few of the middle-aged and elderly) were seeking spiritual empowerment from a guru scorned by the electorate and maligned by the media.
>
> The only science I knew is Religionswissenschaft, as the scientific (historical- analytical) study of religion is called in German. And Nagasena was not an "Aumsatien." He had no knowledge of atoms, unlike the scientists in America who devoted themselves to making the bombs that devastated Hiroshima and Nagasaki.... He had nothing whatsoever to offer to the latest sort of scientific terrorism we have recently witnessed.
>
> What Nagasena did have was an insatiable curiosity about the supernatural, an affinity for esoteric Buddhism, a conviction that he could himself attain liberation if only he tried hard enough. He had absolutely no patience for me whenever I pontificated upon the necessity of being objective, non-committal, and historical in the study of religion....

Nagasena took Young to Aum meetings and introduced him to other Aum members. Young gained a generally favorable impression of what he saw—an electric atmosphere with excited people of all ages studying the "Master's " teachings and practicing their faith. But Young was to learn more about Aum from Nagasena than anything else.

> Next I learned to see Aum Shinrikyo through the eyes of Nagasena's

parents. Mom and Dad, a well-heeled couple stationed abroad with a leading Japanese company, were devastated by their son's announcement of his impending initiation as a monk.Nagasena had just graduated and was killing time before entering a prestigious trading company that most graduates would give their right arm to work for.On several occasions we talked long-distance into the night. The father would lose face; the mother might lose her *ikigai* (reason for living); the son was headed for trouble.I was pleased with myself and thought the compromise I worked out was Solomonic: Encourage him to work for six months, I said, and if it doesn't pan out, let him go his way with your blessing....

Six months later, Nagasena took a part-time job as a custodian at Landmark Tower in Yokohama, where he could be free to devote himself to Aum while keeping off the welfare roles and making a modest contribution to his upkeep at the *dojo* (Aum center).The allure of Toranomon (the Tokyo business district) where he had been working had quickly worn off. It was absolutely the wrong place for a person of his proclivities. Interminable working hours at menial labor had convinced him that he belonged elsewhere.Anyway, he had been unwilling to wait six months, much less a few years, until he could get into the corporate passing lane....

The last time I saw Nagasena, until a week or so after the tragic affair on the Tokyo subways, was shortly before he was to go to Moscow and help establish Aum there.... He kept more than the customary social distance between us; alert to the possibility that my American impulsiveness might prompt me to shake his hand when we said good-bye. Obviously he was afraid of an untoward karmic transfer from me into the body he had worked so hard to purify. When he returned nearly three years later, he had become an "achiever," relaxed enough to eat a dinner of chicken curry with me at an Indian restaurant while pondering to help Aum rise above the public obloquy into which it had fallen.... I knew that he would be an Aum loyalist to the bitter end. He had, I could see, found in the Master a power that filled the void in the bowels of his being.

Nagasena has many of the same characteristics as Murakami's KM. He is much better educated and comes from a wealthy elitist background, but he shares her sense of alienation and hopelessness in a highly materialistic and success-oriented society. He refuses to follow his father's footsteps, but instead devotes his life to Aum because he regards it as the only viable alternative to a life in corporate hell.

Case 2: Akira Sato

Japan Times writer Asako Takaesu interviewed several Aum members immediately after the sarin subway attack including Sato Akira, a male college graduate in his thirties. He describes his first encounter with Sato:

> To my great surprise, Sato entered the reception room at Aum Shinrikyo headquarters casually dressed in a polo shirt and cotton pants. Without the now-familiar white or green garb, this Aum member looked exactly like an average young Japanese. About 170 cm. tall and well-built, Akira is, in fact, "Joe Average." The surprising thing about his life is that it is completely normal for Japan. Therein, perhaps, lies a clue for why the national TV audience is so fascinated with Aum: It is a reflection of Japanese society and a microcosm of all its wishes and anxieties.[5]

Akira grew up in Hokkaido during the 1960s where his father worked as a public service employee. Living in one of the most beautiful and open parts of Japan, Akira had a deep love for nature and spent much of his youth hiking and playing in the woods. Later he attended prestigious Hokkaido University in Sapporo where he first majored in architecture before switching to earthquake engineering. He later got a job as an assistant in a university laboratory.

Although he graduated on schedule, Akira never forgot his love for nature. He joined his university's famous mountain-climbing club and in 1984 spent a year away from Japan on an expedition to the Himalayas. After his ascent team climbed a 6700-meter mountain in northern India, Akira decided to wander through China to Tibet. He was fascinated with the religious atmosphere of Tibet's capital, Lhasa. He had always been interested in religion, Zen Buddhism in particular, but nothing could compare to the surge of enthusiasm that came with the refined Buddhist atmosphere of Tibet.

He returned to Japan with an apparent desire to search for a new way of life. His professional goal of becoming an architect suddenly seemed meaningless to him. Recalling his doubts about architecture, he said:

> What we learn in this field is the pursuit of beauty, but the pursuit of beauty is one of the earthly desires of humanity. Even though art is considered a desire of a higher order, we should rid ourselves of it in order to attain salvation.

Soon after his return he found a book published by Aum Shinrikyo. He recalls being especially impressed with the group's teachings on the concept of Armageddon. "I had always felt that the end of the world is close at hand. With the incredible amount of environmental destruction that's happening on the entire earth, there is no way we can survive unless we change our lifestyle."

Akira belongs to a generation born in the 1960s during Japan's period of most rapid growth, when the nation's air and water were most polluted. He says that some of his earliest memories of tv news were scenes of Minamata, Kyushu, where many victims of mercury poisoning suffered horrible deaths. During his college days, the biological threat of AIDS chilled an entire generation of young people. As a young adult, the Gulf war unleashed the specter of chemical weapons.

> The environmental destruction that is happening today goes far beyond the level of regional pollution, which I grew up hearing a lot about, like Minamata disease. The Collapse of the whole society will one day happen suddenly, just as in physics where a quantum transformation occurs after a long period of subtle changes.

Akira finds the sense of political threats from the rest of the world quite worrisome, especially the needless "Japan-bashing" in trade relations with the United States. He expresses deep misgivings about the endless flood of consumerism coming from America. "Exploitation is going on in the guise of 'free trade.' Japan, for example, is sucking so much out of the developing countries' wealth and does not contribute anything to these countries."

Akira is most concerned with what he thinks is a tendency of the Japanese media to accelerate the nation's cultural decline by promoting hedonistic activities such as "sports, sex, and gourmet dining." He notes that "There is so much greed in the world, too much desire for gourmet food and drink, of which I myself used to devour a lot. The reason we keep wanting these things is because we are not satisfied. I felt as long as we look for happiness outside ourselves, the sense of happiness will always be limited. In order to achieve ultimate happiness, we must go inward.."

Akira thinks Aum attracts young people like himself who have studied science and technology. He insists that science is essentially close to philosophy, especially physics. He notes that the "logical aspects" of Aum's teachings are more accessible and credible to college graduates than the obscure indefinite teachings of more traditional religions. Aum's beliefs are "clear and rational" and therefore "appeal to rationality."

The young convert feels that Aum's training and indoctrination program has had a positive effect on his life. First, the "channels" in his body which had been "blocked" by "impure earthly desires" have become clear. As a result, his nasal problem, called "ozena," from which he had been suffering for years, had been cured. He is also calmer and no longer has major emotional swings as in the past.

Akira feels that the spiritual aspects of Aum have had the most profound effect on his life. After studying the teachings of Asahara and following his instructions for meditation, he says that he has a deep appreciation for the concept of *mujo,* that everything is transient and subject to change. This awareness, in turn, has enabled him to think about the "bigger picture" of life and death.

Meditation also helped him confront past personal problems, which he had tried to suppress, but which have resurfaced time and again. As a result, he has had to come to terms with thee issues and became more mature in the process. The path to such awareness, he believes, comes in measured steps or stages, of gradually increasing *kundalini* energy, manifested in sensory experiences and non-sensory visions. After initial training, he started seeing his past lives and *prana*, an ether-like substance in the air.

Asked how he plans on dealing with the coming Armageddon, so widely predicted by Aum and Asahara, Akira replies that a major goal is "to help bring back the next era of *shoho*." (*Shoho* is the Buddhist term that indicates the time of peace when the teachings of Buddha are followed by society as a whole.) "The present era closely resembles *mappo,*" the Buddhist era of pure evil when society forgets and no longer practices the teachings of Shakyamuni.

Akira views Armageddon as a positive development, a necessary purging of evil where the bad in the world will be eradicated and a new purity will emerge. Akira declares that Asahara is destined to be the leader of a purified peaceful world dominated by Aum.

Akira was as ordinary as any of the devotees discussed in this chapter, but he differed in the sense that he had a clear image of a different life away from Japanese society with all of its pollution and "crass materialism." Aum provided him, it seems, with precisely that alternate way of life he had sought so diligently.

Case 3: Takahashi Hidetoshi

Takahashi Hidetoshi was a 24-year-old geology student at Shinshu University in Nagano Prefecture when he heard a speech by Asahara, who at that time was visiting many colleges hoping to win new recruits. Takahashi had long studied the masters of Western philosophy, but had gained little from his studies. When he asked Asahara about the meaning of life, the Aum leader replied, "Mr. Takahashi, you will not find what you are looking for in your study of science."

Takahashi was so impressed with Asahara that he joined Aum within hours. He later left Aum to study astronomy in graduate school, but he returned to Aum in May 1994. He renounced the world and became a *shukke* thereafter undergoing severe ascetic training and living communally with 1400 other *shukke* in a *satin* (special Aum compound) in a village in Yamanashi Prefecture. He joined Aum's Science and Technology bureau where he worked to develop a computer software named "Astrology of Great Truth."

Takahashi soon found himself completely cut off from the rest of the world. He apparently knew that Aum leaders were lynching some practitioners, but he had no idea that Aum was producing sarin poison gas and only heard of the sarin subway attack several weeks after its occurrence. Only then did he reconsider his affiliation with Aum and leave. He eventually wrote a book *Aum Kara no Kikan* [Coming Back from Aum][6] where he noted:

> Although I have now stopped practicing Aum's asceticism, it once fascinated me very much. It asked me whether I lived in truth or not, and that awoke a search to find my true self by transforming myself. Such a sincere question, asked in conjunction with the asceticism of Aum, offered a hint to the solution I had sought for a long time.Further, the training of Aum was so practical that even my way of breathing was changed. This change produced a good effect in my body. It gave a precise method to the practitioner without thinking about abstract ideas and morals. Such abstraction is sometimes a central dogma in other religious sects. Such direct effects of this practice overwhelmingly attracted us. This was why I was one deeply impressed by Aum's methods.

Takahashi is one of the few people who approached Aum from a strictly intellectual perspective.He sought an ascetic experience that would put him in closer touch with himself. Takahashi sought a *method* to transform himself and thought that he had found it in Aum's form of meditation and practice. Aum served his own purposes very well, but he was at least temporarily unwilling to deal with the whole truth of how Aum treated many of its members and of its overall conduct in society. One wonders how Takahashi and others within Aum could just stand by and do nothing knowing that Aum leaders had killed other members.

Case 4: A Personal Encounter with Aum

This writer's first encounter with Aum members came in Kyoto six weeks after the sarin gassing in Tokyo. I was giving one of my students a personalized tour of downtown Kyoto late one afternoon and was crossing the broad avenue in front of Takashimaya Department Store. I could see a large group of young men and women handing out promotional material and playing lyrical Indian-sounding music from a tape recorder. Huge posters bearing the likeness of Asahara Shoko made it clear that the group belonged to Aum Shinrikyo. Although the group members were trying to pass out promotional material denouncing police tactics and demanding freedom of religious practice, pedestrians literally turned and fled in the other direction to avoid any contact with an Aum member.

I grabbed the opportunity to have a group chat with a small group of the members who were milling around Asahara's poster. After introducing myself as a scholar of Japanese religion, I asked them why they were out on the busiest street corner in Kyoto canvassing on behalf of a man who at the time was the most wanted criminal suspect in Japan.

Their replies were consistent. They were all former college students in the Kyoto area including one from Doshisha University and another from Kyoto University. Several had joined Aum after graduating from school while others had joined and had dropped out of school. They were loyal to Aum and Asahara and had no regrets about their time in the movement. Most, but not all, came from families where their fathers and, in a couple of cases, their mothers had embarked on successful careers. They generally had fond memories of their childhoods—there was no real sense with their being angry with the world. And yet there were few memories of life as a family unit. They were well cared for, but in most cases their fathers were rarely there. Their parents had encouraged them to pursue a higher education, had paid the high cost of *juku* (cram schools), and college tuition and room and board, but there had been little personal involvement in their children's education.

These particular members had entered college, but had felt themselves drifting. They had no serious interests, hobbies or goals. They had not had many childhood encounters with religion, but all remembered being intrigued by Asahara when they first saw his picture, heard one of his videos, read an Aum comic, or actually met him or one of his top recruits. There was a sense of excitement; they felt that Asahara was a man with a purpose who could show them the way to high achievements in their lives.

When I asked them why they had not left after the terrible scandal created by their own leaders, they reacted with a degree of anger, mentioning harassment by police, a menacing press, but they also mentioned matter-of-factly that they had no place to go.

When they made the break from their families, they broke their ties with their former lives.They might have a future direction to head in, but even to try to go back would be denying everything they had done since joining Aum. Aum had given them a new life, however ill-defined it was.

Case 5: Fujii Kiyohiro

Fujii Kiyohiro was a college student from Shimane Prefecture and a devoted Aum member when it published his testimony in the October 1991 issue of *the Mahayana News Letter.*

> So many wonderful things have happened to me since I joined Aum a year ago (1990). Before I entered Aum I was very absent-minded and very lethargic with no direction in life. I would go into prolonged periods of depression. Now I understand that this is because of the impermanence of life. I always had pets, but when they died, especially because of my own negligence, I would feel terrible.
>
> As we look around the world, we can see that killing occurs daily for many trivial reasons. Our world suffers from pollution, the destruction of the environment and even from such past times as fishing. I really want to change this way of life , but I felt so utterly powerless and hated being part of such a world, but I occupied my time with external pleasures and continued on as a student until one day I borrowed an Aum book from a friend.
>
> At that time I despised all religions, but there was something very attractive about Master Asahara. His sermons on the need to get rid of our egos and other afflictions and his dream of building Lotus Villages where the world will some day be a Shambhala (heaven on earth) really made sense. As I learned the teachings of the Truth and performed yoga and other Aum practices after I joined, my pride declined, I was no longer

nervous in the presence of others, and I had a clearer perception of the world.

I lost my anger towards others and was grateful that I could reduce my karma.... I learned that one can attain supernatural powers from Master Asahara and the other monks.

Mr. Fujii was then a student sharing much of the lethargy and boredom of KM and other young members. Life had no real meaning, so he drifted along like a log floating n a sluggish stream. He sensed that the world around him was not in good shape. It was only when he finally entered Aum that he found a sense of purpose.

Category III: Aum's Academics

Asahara and Aum Shinrikyo attracted a surprisingly large group of scholars, scientists, doctors, lawyers, and people trained in various advanced technologies (see previous chapter). Some of these younger academics were attracted by teachings, which claimed to be both religious and scientific. This tendency ran contrary to their academic training, which placed a clear barrier between religion and science. One Aum leader wrote: "Buddhism is a science because it explains things in life logically. Buddhist teachings are supported with logic and logic should explain any kind of phenomena. This is the view of Master Asahara."

Case 1: A Scholarly Attraction

Aum attracted a surprisingly large number of students and young scholars including graduates of and graduate students enrolled at Tokyo University. Academic life attracts many people because it emphasizes the freedom to think and to develop the mind as one sees fit. But academic life in Japan can be very restrictive which is perhaps a reason why Aum attracted a number of academic.

The New York Times and *The Washington Post* both ran stories in late April 1995 about a brilliant young PhD candidate in his late twenties who had quit a job in a major trading company to return to graduate school. His thesis topic was on the history and theology of Aum, but when he began contacting Aum members and leaders, he became entranced with the movement and soon joined. He told reporters that he had had no interest in the materialistic world of business.

Later the student found inspiration in the teachings and meditative practices of Aum and Asahara, whom he continued to admire even after the gas attack. "I admire the supreme master because he tells us things so clearly and logically." He remembers how during one intense meditation session that he saw his research papers tossed and scattered into the air. "I felt as if I had ascended to a higher stage. A bright light fell from above and entered me."[7]

Academic life in itself can be as empty and devoid of meaning as any other profession. Asahara was an anti-hero who defied conventional authority and openly challenged the assumptions of a materialistic society. This young scholar entertained a strong distaste for the world of business and finance and eschewed the benefits that a doctorate from Tokyo University could have brought him. The lack of any sense of spiritualism led him to Aum and a sense of satisfaction in life.

Case 2: Sasaki Masamitsu

Sasaki Masamitsu is one of a group of young doctors who joined Aum. He was a 32-year-old neurologist from Okayama when he submitted this testimony to Aum's *Mahayana Newsletter in 1991.*

> It was my encounter with Asahara's book *Supreme Initiation* that led me to the Truth in June 1987. I had reached a standstill with the six years of practice at Agonshu. I saw no change in myself nor did I have any mystic experiences. On the contrary, I felt that my worldly passions had increased.
>
> Soon after I became a member of Aum in August 1987, I had the awakening of Kundalini and various other mystic experiences. I am now certain that I was a disciple of the Master in one or more of my former lives.
>
> One of the blessings I received from Aum is the cure of my duodenal ulcer. I had suffered from annual relapses of this painful disease for over a decade. I would suddenly have a severe pain in my upper stomach and would have to take medicine to ease the pain. But when I had the relapse again in September two years ago, I decided to cure it by Gaja Kalani.

Sasaki went through a rigorous series of steps prescribed by Asahara that led to a complete cure.

I am a doctor and I know very well that a medicine such as an antacid can give immediate relief from pain, but it is, so to say, only covering up the bad spot. Unless one's karma is rightly adjusted, the problem is not really solved.

NowI have a problem of my own. As a doctor I specialize in neurology and deal with patients with diseases such as cerebral apoplexy, Parkinson's disease, muscular dystrophy, and cervical spondylosis, diseases for which there are no definite cures. I feel keenly the limits of Western medicine and the powerlessness of a doctor.

But, as a doctor working for a public hospital, I am not in the position to openly preach Dharma to my patients. I consider it part of my duty to use the energy which I have preserved with my practice and through the empowerment (of Aum practice).But it is frustrating because the precious energy is not effectively used for the spreading of the dharma. I am trying my best with Mahayanic spirit telling myself it is a practice of Dharma offering...

For such reasons I am thinking of becoming a monk and working in Aum's Astral hospital when the time comes (Right now I have all of my family and relatives against me.....).

This case demonstrates the importance of physical duress as a reason for joining a new religion. In this case, however, we find a highly trained doctor who, one might imagine, might have a medical solution to his problems. But like Dr. Hayashi, the heart surgeon mentioned earlier who is serving a life-sentence for his participation in the sarin gas attack, Dr. Sasaki was seeking a deeper sense of morality and religiosity. Even being a doctor can be mundane work for some, and Aum appeared to fill that spiritual void in their lives.

Category IV: Older Members

Although Aum has been categorized as primarily a "youth movement," it always had a respectable number of middle-aged and elderly members, especially during its early years.There were a few elderly men who joined, but most older members were women, most of them housewives or widows who felt alone in life. There were also a few younger women who joined as well.

Shortly after the Tokyo sarin gas incident, there were news reports of two older women who lived together in a room in one of Asahara's compounds. They expressed considerable confusion over the turmoil and all of the negative comments concerning Asahara in the press. They told reporters that they had formerly lived by themselves, alone and forgotten. When they somehow encountered Asahara, he brought them to an Aum residence, gave them a room, and personally cared for them. One of the women recalls telling Asahara that she was cold at night and that he personally provided her with a blanket and covered her himself. They openly wondered how such a warm and kind man could possibly be accused of such violent crimes. They cherished Asahara as a long lost son who had saved them from the misery and loneliness of old age.

There were several other elderly people living in Aum compounds in 1995. Most of them had joined Aum in the mid-1980s when it was a small yoga group and several of them had left Agonshu with Asahara in 1984. By 1995 Aum had become their only home and they were without any contacts in the "real" world. An older woman wrote in the late 1980s:

> Before joining Aum I was always afraid of showing my real self to other people and was always conscious of other peoples' eyes. I was always hiding myself because I wanted other people to have a better image of me or not dislike me....I was never free from worries....

After a brief conversation with Asahara, she said, "He understands me better than I do myself and he always gives me the right advice."[8]

Case 1: The Piano of the Mind

Kanako is a former professional pianist, trained in classical music who joined Aum at first because she was a musician deeply impressed with Aum's affinity for dance and music. She was born into a Buddhist family in Shimane Prefecture, where her grandfather was chief priest at a temple. While in high school she began to read many books on philosophy to determine the meaning of life and the destiny of mankind. She had little respect for people pursuing happiness through money and fame: "I thought to myself that there must be some more noble purpose in life. Since the piano offered an avenue for personal development, she went to music school and years later became a respected and successful musician. However, she eventually reached a level of skill or ceiling that she could not surpass. Some critics said that her music lacked "vitality."

Kanoko was searching for answers and felt that she might find them in

Aum Shinrikyo. She was attracted to Aum's claim in a book that one could find supernatural power step-by-step through a series of spiritual training exercises. After reading Aum literature for over a year, she joined the group as an affiliated lay member who attended Aum functions, but who lived at home. She rapidly felt refreshed and renewed and her music seemed to have a new vitality.

Aum's teaching, she says, has had profound and numerous effects on her life. Physically, she feels much more energetic since her conversion. She recalls tiring easily and always feeling weak, but she claims that kundalini energy has been released to flow through the channels in her body which have been cleared by training. She feels that this new energy is also manifest in her music.

The most rewarding aspect of her relationship with Aum, she says, is not her music, but, rather, her increased spirituality. Through training, she claims to have been able to elevate herself to a higher state. She recalls that in Buddhism there are many layers of existence above the human condition, which is ranked fourth from the bottom. Those with a higher degree of spirituality emit an energy field, which gives others a sense of security and a feeling of happiness. Thus, she feels, by attaining such a spiritual level, she hopes that she will be able to help others indirectly. And, eventually, direct assistance can be given by teaching others to eliminate impure thoughts and elevating themselves to a higher state.

Like other Aum members, Kanako agrees with Aum's belief in impending Armageddon. She feels that the world is heading deeper into a state of *mappo*. "Crimes and bullying are rampant, and people are behaving egotistically, not caring about others. People seem to be seeking only momentary pleasures and material possessions. Asked what she would do after global annihilation, she replied enigmatically , "Whether Armageddon comes or not, I would like to continue to train myself and become spiritually advanced so that my very existence would have a positive influence on others."

Kanako, unlike some other members introduced here, was primarily attracted by Aum's claims that its members could enhance their strength to the extent of becoming "supermen." She was only a mundane piano player, but she hoped to use this strength to leap frog beyond her very ordinary career.

Case 2: Takeshita Hiroko[9]

Takeshita Hiroko (pseudonym), like so many younger members of her generation, was very ambivalent about her life. She was not terribly enthusiastic about living in Japan and following a traditional Japanese career path. She dated an American English instructor, Steve Reynolds (pseudonym), for three years both in Japan and the United States before marrying him in 1991 and moving to the United States in 1992.

Unbeknownst to Steve, Hiroko had joined Aum for a brief period before going to America. Initially, she was not an enthusiastic member. She quit after a few months, but rejoined Aum while in the US. She called Aum's New York office once a week for "consultation" on yoga, meditation, and prescribed reading. A modest monthly fee of $18 and limited obligations had little effect on the marriage initially, but before long Steve suspected that there was more to her involvement when Hiroko began to curb sexual activities—Aum taught that energy expended in sex would interfere with her practice of Kundalini yoga by dissipating her energy. Hiroko accompanied Asahara on a pilgrimage to India and was an enthusiastic member when the couple moved back to Japan in early 1993.

Hiroko's increased involvement with Aum gradually led to bitter quarrels between her and her husband. Hiroko complained about Steve's lack of support and cooperation in her practice while Steve complained about her excessive devotion to the group, the strange beliefs and practices she now espoused, and the karmic interpretations she put to all occurrences. Hiroko became convinced she felt other peoples' karma, which surfaced as various pains throughout her body. Even though Steve considered himself an open-minded agnostic, he found her spiritual interpretations as absurd: "I imagined her becoming a Moonie or one of those strange people standing at the train stations wanting to pray for you."

The marriage deteriorated to the state that both began discussing divorce, but Steve, despite his skepticism over Aum, decided to play for time by joining in some Aum activities.He took part in various training programs, initiations and "shaktipat," where Asahara or one of his leaders would rub the initiate's forehead, transferring in "clean energy." All Steve remembers happening is feeling continually ill.

Steve was shocked at the huge sums of money that Aum demanded from them. Hiroko's parents had given them 8 million yen (about $80,000 at the time) as a wedding gift, but before long the entire amount had gone to Aum. Even such brief encounters as Shaktipat cost them $500.

Steve grew increasingly concerned and angry about their involvement with Aum. One factor that drew his attention was the "yogic interpretations of reality." "What was the weirdest about this whole experience was the way I started to accept certain things as normal—like conversations about Armageddon at dinner.

Hiroko spent a few months in late 1993 and early 1994 working in the Aum office in Moscow under adverse conditions. She would have stayed longer, but Steve flew to Russia and persuaded her to return home. After their return Hiroko began spending long stretches of time at an Aum compound. Her behavior became increasingly strange by early 1995. She became paranoid and had bad memory lapses. She moved to Tokyo to run an Aum translation bureau just at the time of the sarin gas attack. She found herself followed and frequently questioned by police. When Steve tried to persuade her to leave Aum, Steve remembers, "She lost herself, she was paranoid, etc. Suddenly she quit Aum and within a few days ran away, convinced that I was a spy." Steve returned to California, but failed to resume any career there. His friends and colleagues shunned him because of his involvement with Aum.

When Steve met Hiroko two months after their separation, he found that she had regained her composure. She had quit Aum and had thrown way all of her Aum paraphernalia. But she told her husband that she wanted a complete break with the past, including him. She wanted a divorce and a chance to live in solitude like a monk. She talked of going to India and joining a monastery.

Steve and Hiroko had survived their encounter with Aum without any physical damage, but the emotional and financial toll was immense. Aum had destroyed their marriage, set back or ruined their careers, and taken all their money. They lost all hope for a happy life and became lonely, directionless and embittered people. Hiroko's experience also draws attention to the fact that even after several years as an active member of Aum, her ambiguous view of life continued and she kept on with her life of listless wandering.

Asahara Shoko is a charismatic leader who keenly understood the psychological and physical needs of many Japanese. Aum Shinrikyo grew in strength and popularity in the late 1980s at a time when Japan had reached the height of its postwar prosperity and before the economic "bubble" burst in 1991.The nation's astounding prosperity brought success to millions of Japanese, but there were many victims as well.Young-to-middle-aged housewives left at home alone often suffered from deep depression and a sense of loneliness. Younger-less-educated workers who had to work long hours under bad conditions for a low salary sought for something more meaningful—perhaps a sense of power or a realm where they too could be supermen. College students or recent graduates encountered a Japan where the "corporate rat race" was the key to success. Many of them wanted a different way to spend their lives, an alternative way to happiness and even power.

Author Murakami Haruki summarized the situation best when he noted that Aum was born out of a condition of "extraordinary ordinariness." There is little that distinguishes any of the twelve people introduced above from millions of other "ordinary" Japanese. They lived in average homes, had adequate incomes, were popular with members of the opposite sex, and had the potential for success in corporate Japan. But, even though they were all seemingly in good shape, they could tell Murakami, "We felt as if there was a gaping hole in our bodies; our hearts were cold."

Murakami correctly notes that there is no constructive, normal subsocial system in Japan which can absorb people who cannot or will not function in mainstream society.Richard Young's young friend Nagasena sought an alternative to the materialistic daily grind of corporate Japan, but the failure of his parents to truly understand him as an individual and the failure of society to offer him an adequate escape route made him susceptible to the "Lotus Village" propaganda expounded by Asahara and his henchmen.

These followers of Aum joined because they believed that Aum offered them a new, meaningful, productive and *peaceful* way of life. There is little indication that in its early years Asahara and other Aum leaders meant to betray them, the most loyal of their followers, but in the end, they did. Asahara left them stranded without help or resources. Metaphorically, he had offered them a loving relationship, but in the end he had ravished them instead.

Chapter VII

ಸಾಶ

The Farce of the "Great Russian Salvation Tour" and Ventures Elsewhere

A t the time of the Tokyo sarin gas incident in 1995, the Japanese media overwhelmed the public with its coverage of Aum's activities in Japan, where Aum allegedly had ten thousand supporters, but made little mention of its 30,000[1] followers in Russia. Except for a few journalistic accounts, Japan and the West have received very little information about what is surely one of the most interesting meetings between Japanese and Russians in many years.

Asahara made three trips to Russia in 1992-93 accompanied by as many as 270 faithful from Japan on chartered Aerflot jets.[2] Aum ran a fully-staffed main office in Moscow and four branch offices elsewhere in Russia. Asahara and other Aum leaders initially were well received by a number of ranking Kremlin leaders as well as by many ordinary Russians. Aum bought extensive blocks of time on Russian television and radio and broadcast many of Asahara's speeches and workshops throughout Russia as well as regular broadcasts to Japan beamed via Vladivostock. We also know that Aum clandestinely bought a Russian military helicopter and other equipment from the Russian black market but failed in its attempt to acquire materials for nuclear weapons.[3]

Aum media reports that Asahara first visited Russia in March 1992 with 270 supporters in response to a November 1991 invitation from the

Russian Republic.[4] Asahara gave lectures at Moscow University and six other universities[5], made several appearances on Russian television and radio, addressed a few groups of several thousand Russians at "initiation ceremonies," and met with a number of "influential" Russian politicians.

Aum claims that as a result of the three "Russian Salvation Tours," "seven out of ten people on the streets of Moscow say that they have heard of Aum Shinrikyo and Master Asahara."[6] A steady stream of 200 or more Russians visited the main or branch offices of Aum on a daily basis and in 1992 and 1993 there were days when 100 or more new members signed up. Each Aum office reportedly bustled with activity every day and night.

One Aum staffer from Japan wrote:

> These days, many people in Moscow are joining Aum. People who have learned about Master Asahara through television, radio, leaflets, and posters visit my office continuously. In my branch alone, one hundred people became members in one day.
>
> I admonish new members by saying to them that it isn't helpful that only they are saved after they hear the Master's Lectures. So, later, they take people to the branch one after another, and in this way many people enter Aum....Many people who have become members have practiced other religious teachings, like yoga, etc. But none of them have come across the real thing. Aum has a perfect system of practice, the perfect law—everything is perfect. People realize this and enter Aum when it is revealed to them.[7]

Why Did Aum Appeal to so Many Russians?

Russia has a long and very strong Christian tradition and, thus, many writers in the West are puzzled as to why thirty-thousand Russians, many of them very well educated, joined Aum. There are various interpretations.

Aum credits its radio and television broadcasts as well as the charisma of Asahara and the greatness of his teachings. Endorsements of Aum by Russians indicate that an overwhelming number of new members first heard of Aum through the media. Aum also credits its great success to the disruption of life in Russia after the fall of the Soviet Union. "Many Russians are striving to make a living now and are suffering mentally from the confusion of the collapse of communism. Many believe that the practices and teachings of AUM Shinrikyo promise true happiness...."[8]

Anybody who walks the streets of Moscow and St. Petersburg these days will see isolated examples of new wealth—a fancy car or a new boutique—but the main sight is a sense of sadness and desperation in the eyes of many others. The fall of communism led to hyper-inflation where the value of the Russian ruble fell from a few rubles to the dollar to 5,000 to a dollar (1996). People on fixed salaries and pensions saw their livelihoods destroyed. A parallel breakdown in authority has led to increased anxiety and considerable criminal activity.

Russian churches I visited on Sundays in 1996 were packed with many generally older Russians. Younger Russians grew up under a Soviet regime that strongly discouraged religious practice. According to reports I read in the Russian media, younger Russians, like their counterparts in Japan, rarely take part in traditional Christian activities, but are still seeking a new sense of spirituality.

Russians have often turned to mystics during periods of stressful transition. All students of Russian history are aware of the powerful presence of Rasputin in the years before the Russian Revolution. Rasputin, the "mystic from the East," convinced many members of the royal family of his faith healing powers. In recent years other "gurus" have drawn even bigger audiences in Russia and eastern Europe. A few years ago a faith healer, Anatoly Kashpirovsky, drew tens of millions of television viewers when he promised to perform a live operation on a woman using his healing powers to keep her out of pain. Shortly before his fall, President Mikhail Gorbachev welcomed controversial Korean Unification Church leader Sun Myung Moon to the Kremlin and allowed "Moonies" to perform a ritual in a Kremlin Cathedral. Many fundamentalist churches in the United States have sent missionaries to Russia. Thus, Asahara was only one in a parade of foreign religions leaders and "mystics" that have met some degree of success in Russia since the mid-1980s.

Statements by Russian converts in Aum publications indicate that a Russian orchestra organized by Aum, "Chyren" (Sanskrit for "divine offering"), drew a lot of favorable attention from Russians. According to AERA, Aum offered to pay up to $1,000 a month to skilled Russian musicians to join his new orchestra. A thousand dollars is very high for a Russian musician and many of them rushed to audition for Chyren.[9] The new orchestra played Aum-derived "Astral music" as well as more traditional fare at Aum convocations and on television and radio and sold tapes and CDs of their music.

Asahara's own speeches and presentations also attracted a large number of curious Russians. Perhaps Asahara's greatest coup consisted of invitations to speak at major Russian universities. One of the talks, "How do Mental

Illusions Occur?" focused on the lack of brain wave activity in enlightened beings such as himself, the Buddha, and Jesus (see chapter 2). Using a blend of pseudo-science and his own religious beliefs, Asahara sought to convince his audience that the way to perfect enlightenment is a complete transformation of the personality. Once this occurs, a person's *normally high brain activity becomes very calm.* "My EEG record shows that my brain waves have a frequency below 0.05 hertz. Doctors say that it is an inconceivable phenomenon that I am alive and talking to you today. They say that I should be dead. But this is the state in which the primary projection of the deepest level of consciousness manifests in this world most accurately. In other words, I have the cleanest mirror. This state is described in Buddhist texts as 'the state of a Buddha who has attained mirror-like wisdom....' I am leading a regular life deeper than what is normally considered deep sleep. This sense of calm is only found in Buddhas"[10].

Aum's Shallow Roots in Mother Russia

One must question the actual strength of Aum Shinrikyo in Russia despite its claims of 30,000 members. Conversion to a new religion requires more than signing one's names to a piece of paper and attending two or three meetings. Aum regarded the *shukkesha* as the core of its movement. Aum as a faith renounces society and teaches that one can only transform oneself through renunciation and active practice. By 1995 there were over 1,100 Aum renunciates in Japan which gave Aum a strong base. But conflicting reports from Aum put the number of "monks" in Russia at only 50 or 170, a tiny fraction of the claimed membership.[11]

Such a small core indicates that although Aum made a successful entry on to the Russian scene, it failed to develop a strong base in its three years there.[12] Aum in Russia seems little more than a passing fad that quickly disappeared except for a small handful of members who seriously sought to devote themselves Asahara's new teachings. The experience of one of Aum's Russian monks, Marina Romandina, is recounted in Kaplan and Marshall's *The Cult at the End of the World.*[13]

Marina was an eighteen-year old blond student taking time off from a Moscow-area music college when she first encountered Aum in 1993. She found Asahara's teachings to be so stimulating that she decided to become a "monk." She shaved off her hair, devoured books by Asahara and moved into an Aum commune in Moscow. She repeated the vow, "I am happy to join Aum. I will always follow the guru. I will become a monk" repeatedly each day. There were two three-hour breaks for sleep and a ritual called "sacrificing food to the guru." "We had to eat until we felt sick. This was to make us understand that food caused pain. Anyone who threw up had to eat their own vomit."

Marina gradually suspected there was more to Aum's daily regimen of two meals of macaroni and porridge. She remembers feeling strange after each meal. "After eating, I always felt sleepy and had vivid dreams." She suspects that she was being drugged. Then there were the pills. "Every month we were given a package of small yellow tablets called 'sattva vitamins.' We took one every day. Afterwards, I'd feel so lethargic. I couldn't think....I didn't want to think." She has reason to believe that the "vitamins" were actually a type of prescription tranquilizer called Fenozepan.

Life in the Moscow Aum community center deteriorated rapidly. Russian Aum members suffered chronic health problems. "Just about everyone was suffering from some kind of neurosis. Monks beat each other up. Women quarreled the whole time. There was a lot of talk of suicide." Life in a supposedly utopian commune had become pure hell. "It was hard for me to think rationally. Nobody was in control of themselves anymore. Many of us had high temperatures and allergies. My throat ached and my eyes watered." When Marina began smelling strange chemical odors and getting terrible headaches, she fled.

Marina survived her encounter with Aum, but others were not so lucky. A young Russian male member hung himself from a tree branch in a Moscow park without any explanation. A thirteen-year old who joined with his mother jumped to his death from a balcony of a Moscow apartment after endless taunts from other "monks" who criticized his "lack" of spiritual progress. A few other former Aum members are still missing.

As was the case in Japan, Aum approached people suffering from depression and searching for a panacea to end their misery. Asahara arrived on the scene with promises, but he abandoned and hurt his followers just as he had done in Japan.

Aum's Relationship with Russian Leaders

Asahara and other Aum leaders seemed to have had unusually close access to Russian leaders, but Aum was not the only Japanese religious group to enjoy such privileges. As previously noted, the Rev. Moon, head of Korea's Unification Church, once visited Moscow on an invitation from President Gorbachev. Japan's Soka Gakkai has enjoyed a cordial relationship with Soviet / Russian leaders since the 1970s, long before the Gakkai had become a mainstream group acceptable to Japan's establishment. The Gakkai has few if any members in Russia and has never launched any major proselytization campaigns among the Russian people. But Soka Gakkai chief Ikeda Daisaku and other Gakkai leaders have traveled to Moscow on many occasions to meet Kremlin leaders as well as other ranking Russian cultural and intellectual luminaries. Students at Soka Gakkai schools in Japan have had exchange visits with Russian students. Soka University has an active exchange program with Moscow University.

Since the Soka Gakkai has never actively sought many converts in Russia, one wonders what each side saw in the other. Officially, the Gakkai delegations are "Missions of Peace" to strengthen ties between Russians and Japanese. A cynic, however, might remark that a picture in a Gakkai publication of Ikeda meeting Gorbachev at some important Russian landmark adds legitimacy and prestige to the Gakkai. Russian leaders might utilize the Gakkai's close ties with many Japanese leaders for their own benefit. Neither side ever mentions money, but cash-starved Russians might benefit from a few Gakkai contributions. When I visited a Gakkai book store in Nagoya in June, 1997, I found a book containing a dialogue between ikeda and Gorbachev. Since the Gakkai has always been generous to outside writers who publish under their banner, it is easy to see why Gorbachev, who no longer has a government income, might publish a book with Ikeda.

Perhaps Russian leaders expected Asahara to be another Ikeda. When Asahara visited Moscow the first time in March, 1992, he was scheduled to meet President Yeltsin, but Yeltsin cancelled the visit and Asahara had to settle for Russian Vice-President Aleksandr Rutskoi. Moscow University faculty and staff gave a warm welcome to Asahara, who made a donation of $80,000 of computers.[14]

But one powerful Moscow politician, Oleg Lobov, head of Russia's Security Council, immediately befriended Asahara. Lobov's pet scheme was a Russia-Japan University in Moscow. The Russian government gave him a large old Moscow building, but no staff, faculty, or equipment. Lobov was having problems raising much money in Japan until he met the cash-carrying head of Aum. Sadly for Lobov, his ties with Aum made it impossible to get money from any other Japanese sources and when Aum died in 1995, so did his university.[15]

Asahara also spent lavishly elsewhere. He paid dearly for access to

Russian television and radio. Aum's top man in Russia next to Asahara, Hayakawa Kiyohide, allegedly devoted a great deal of time and money exploring Russia's large market in advanced weapons. A nuclear bomb worth $15 million was on his wish list. If a bomb were not available, he hoped to purchase highly radioactive material that Aum could use to build its own bomb in Japan. No official source has revealed how close Aum came to getting or manufacturing a nuclear bomb, but Aum did manage to purchase a Russian military helicopter.[16]

Aum's sudden collapse in March 1995 in Tokyo also led to its demise in Moscow. Russian police raided Aum headquarters and branch offices, froze its assets, and detained as many of its leaders as they could find.

Aum Activities in the United States

American congressional investigators announced in late October, 1995 that Aum had bought American computer software and air filtering systems that could be used to make chemical and biological weapons and that it had recruited at least two Russian nuclear scientists. Other attempts to buy sophisticated American equipment including a 50 million yen ($US 500,000) laser system and 400 Israeli-made gas masks had failed.[17]

Aum set up a sophisticated purchasing network in the United States that included an office in New York and a freight consolidating agent in California. The New York office was disguised as a religious center where Aum instructors taught various yoga and meditation classes and worshippers could meditate while listening to taped chanting. Some efforts were made to recruit American members, but it is said that only a small handful— perhaps no more than two or three dozen New Yorkers—made the "ultimate donation" by giving Aum all of their assets and becoming full devotees.[18] The New York headquarters was the center used by Aum officials in attempts to procure American equipment.

The New York office had worked hard to purchase two American laser systems. One, normally used in measuring optical lenses, could also be used to measure spheres of plutonium. The New York office also received a computer for a thirty-day trial with American software used in designing pharmaceuticals, but the group later returned the computer to the manufacturer without the hard drive that holds the software.

One of Aum's American followers, "David," sounded strikingly like some of his Japanese counterparts when Nippon Television interviewed him in 1995. "David," a nineteen-year-old religious studies major at Columbia University, stated that he believed in "...Armageddon, in the sense that there will be a catastrophic war between the United States and Japan, that the U.S. will attack Japan, and the world will go into chaos." The coming apocalypse, he added was "purification of the karma." How did he feel about Asahara, the reporter asked.

> "He's the person I respect the most."
> "Which part of him?"
> "His desire to end the suffering of all beings in the universe, to sacrifice his own happiness, his own peace of mind, and give that peace to other individuals."[19]

Aum in Western Australia[20]

Aum's brief excursion into Australia in the fall of 1993 was clearly not for religious purposes. There were never any converts or any form of proselytization. The only Aum base was the abandoned and decayed Banjawarn sheep station in the remote hinterlands of Western Australia, 600 kilometers northwest of Perth. To this day it is not entirely clear why Aum bought the Banjawarn station, why its leaders spent so very little time there, and what they actually did there. One problem is that all Aum members had one-month tourists visas which Australian authorities vowed not to reissue for six months when they caught Aum officials trying to sneak various illegal chemicals past customs officials. Time was not on Aum's side in the Outback.

There are three plausible reasons for Aum's purchase of land in Australia. Aum may have hoped to mine enough uranium to manufacture a nuclear weapon if it failed to purchase one in Russia, but Aum members found little if any during their brief stay there. There is circumstantial evidence that Aum experimented with the manufacture of sarin gas and used it to kill up to 29 hapless sheep. Aum also may have been looking for a remote safe refuge, but this plan was stymied by Australia's refusal to provide additional visas.

Two Aum leaders, Hayakawa Kiyohide and Inoue Yoshihiro, arrived in Perth in April 1993 and immediately contacted an Australian real estate agent of Japanese origin. They spent the next few days flying around Western Australia to several sheep stations to inspect them as prospective locations to establish a sect facility. At each stop the two Aum leaders went off by themselves for several hours with boxes containing electronic testing equipment to which probes were attached for inserting in the ground. They finally decided to purchase Banjawarn Station and returned home. The 190,000 hectare property cost them A$540,000 (about US$400,000). The Aum leaders also engaged an Australian mining resources consultant to obtain mineral exploration licenses for A$150,000 ($US 113,000) to make sure that nobody else could enter the property to prospect for minerals. They also formed two Aum-owned companies, Mahaposya Australia Pty Ltd and Clarity Investments Pty Ltd which in turn became the actual holders of the mineral exploration licenses.

A twenty-five person Aum contingent including Asahara flew to Perth and then to Banjawarn Station on 9 September 1993. They had to pay a whopping A$30,000 for excess-luggage which included a lot of mining equipment. Australian customs officers in Perth also found a whole array of chemicals including hydrochloric acid and perchloric acids in large glass jars labeled "hand soap." Two sect members, Endo Seiichi and Nakagawa Tomomasa, were charged with carrying dangerous goods aboard an aircraft and fined A$2,400 (US $1,800).

Asahara and the majority of his team only stayed in Australia for a short period before returning to Tokyo, and the rest of the team remained only until 4 October. Asahara and his key followers were never able to return to Australia because the Australian embassy refused to issue them new visas because of the suspicious nature of their first mission. Two members managed to get back to Australia to act as caretakers for the Banjawarn station by getting visas from the Australian consulate in Osaka. But there was virtually no Aum activity at Banjawarn after October 1993 and the station was sold to other investors in 1994.

The big mystery is why Aum came to Australia in the first place. When the news of the sarin gas attack in Tokyo reached Western Australia in March, 1995, the new owners of Banjawarn Station called Australian Federal Police to investigate some strange findings at the station. There were traces of a highly organized chemistry laboratory in the kitchen of an abandoned house on the station. Samples of residue in a drain identified the presence of methylphosphonic acid (MPA), a residue of the nerve gas sarin.

Near the homestead police found twenty-nine sheep carcasses as well as a large amount of chemicals such as hydrochloric, perchloric and nitric acids, which are often used for soil assaying and can be used for the simple nerve gas phosgene. There was no evidence of any sarin. There was evidence, however, of MPA in the soil and in some of the sheep carcasses. However, if one is to prove definitively the presence of sarin, chemists need to find evidence of yet another chemical by-product, isophyl methyl-phosphonic acid (IMPA), but the equipment used at the site was not strong enough to find small traces of IMPA.

The logical assumption is that Aum leaders came to Australia to develop sarin gas and that they had tested the sarin on the sheep, but there is no conclusive, only circumstantial, evidence of this. Some of the sheep inexplicably had been bludgeoned to death. There are also reports that Aum came to Australia to mine for uranium deposits—they brought plenty of mining equipment with them—but it is difficult to determine whether they did any mining and, if so, if they found anything at all. All that is known for certain is that Aum spent a lot of money to acquire land and mining licenses, experimented with a variety of chemical agents and killed a number of sheep after spending only a very little time there.

According to some Aum followers, Asahara felt that isolated Australia would be one of the few places that would be relatively unaffected by the impending Armageddon, thus making it an ideal place to establish a permanent facility. However, the failure of Aum top brass to get re-entry visas made it impossible for Aum to establish any base there. But the intriguing mystery of why Aum went to Australia has yet to be answered.

A neighboring group of aborigines who passed by the station while Aum members were still there reported seeing a very strange sight. Phyllis Thomas, leader of the Mulga Queen Aboriginal settlement fifty kilometers away told Reuters:

> We saw four or five people wearing white or cream protective clothing or helmets. They were standing next to a light plane. I think it was twin-engined, and there were some other people in the plane. I was frightened. I thought they looked like wild, savage people. I thought to myself, they're doing something they're not supposed to be doing.[21]

Aum Activities Elsewhere

David Kaplan reports that Aum had a tiny office in Bonn Germany that attracted even fewer members than in New York.[22] Asahara visited Sri Lanka in 1991 and a year later Aum had purchased a tea plantation that it wanted to transform into a "Lotus Village," but even though Aum developed ties with Sri Lanka's president, its efforts failed there as well. Asahara and his entourage visited China in early 1994, but received a cold reception. Similar missions to Taiwan ended in failure.

Aum may have had further plans for foreign operations, but the growing crisis in Japan forced Aum to concentrate on the home front.

Chapter VIII

ഇയരു

Conclusion

The macabre, surreal self-destructive violence of Aum Shinrikyo in 1995 is a chilling reminder of the lengths to which people will go to find a viable meaning and value system and a sense of community—something to believe in and somewhere to belong. Starving for meaning and companionship in life, some people will go to great extremes to find a suitable physical and mental dwelling.[1]

Tragically, there are often complex persons like Asahara Shoko who claim to meet their needs. Asahara fits the stereotype of the excessive religious "cult" leader—charismatic, grandiose, and ultimately quite paranoid. Unable to connect with more traditional religions or milder New Religions, Aum disciples embraced a "bad religion," a rather perverse caricature of what a more positive and healthy faith might have brought them.

Personally peripheral in their lives and having a sour image of more traditional engagements, the Aum brotherhood had found a sense of inclusion and a ready-made answer to their questions and complaints. The Aum community offered them a reassuring and redeeming corporate rationale for each individual's long-standing sense of marginality.

Unfortunately, Aum offered little that ultimately was reassuring or helpful to many of its members. Robert Kisala notes:

What is truly tragic...is that Aum repeats and intensifies many of the cultural forms it criticizes. It postpones the promised empowerment, makes authority absolute, and keeps believers in the dark regarding their leader's true plans. Comparisons have been made with the Japanese Red Army of the 1970s, another radical protest group that copied internally the patterns of power that it sought to destroy in society at large. These groups serve to reflect back to a society its least appealing features—it is little wonder that society wants to treat them as aberrations.[2]

Aum portrayed itself as a Buddhist movement and used a lot of its terminology, but in practice there was a stunning absence of altruism, a total lack of compassion and respect for the dignity of life found in true Buddhism and other mainstream religions. The Buddhist Bodhisattva opts to postpone his achievement of Nirvana to serve as a pilgrim teacher. Jesus resolves to save mankind before remaining in Heaven forever.

Aum's young membership chose to flee society and much of the social responsibility for their narcissistic life in an isolated community. Their youth, intelligence and energy could have been used to solve some of the social abuses they sought to avoid. Individually they appear to have started out as quite decent people who could have served society rather than trying to destroy it.

Morioka Masahiro (b. 1958), currently a researcher in ethics, wrote a book[3] concerning the involvement or interest of youth in Aum. He was formerly a science student, but abandoned his studies because, he contends, science provided little help in his quest to find greater meaning in life. Since he himself had had considerable experience with mysticism, he was anxious to acquire a kind of super power claimed by Asahara. He wrote: "If you do not understand this kind of mystical, occult mentality spreading in the young generation, you cannot grasp the true meaning of the Aum problem."[4]

Morioka shows sympathy for Aum youths who sought "salvation and recovery of the soul." These young people, however, erred when they surrendered themselves into artificial groups which promised a "package deal" of salvation and recovery of the soul. He suggests that they should have taken a far more pro-active rather than a passive stance. Rather than waiting to be saved by some "know-it-all" guru, they should be brave enough to endure this struggle on their own. Morioka cautions that we must pay very close attention to those who have experienced (or who expressed an interest) in Aum to see "how they will live from tomorrow."

Ironically, traditional Buddhism stresses self-empowerment and freedom from suffering through a process of internal change and a search for wisdom. The Eight-Fold path combines the need for external morality and a cleansing of the heart—a parallel process that led Ebenezer Scrooge to transform himself in Dickens' classic. A Buddhist learns that he cannot transform the outside world, but he can alter the way that he perceives and relates to it.

There is a genuine despair among many younger Japanese today. The questions raised by Aum and other new Japanese religious movements about what Murakami Haruki calls the "evils" of Japanese society are very legitimate, but in the case of Aum, its followers made a tragic leap from "the frying pan into the fire." New religions in contemporary Japan express the same hope for the future as many young people: a savior who can save them from the spiritual poverty of modern times.

Honest Buddhism stresses that the only hope for renewal lives within ourselves. Young Japanese must not eschew politics—they must participate actively in the political process championing the cause of reform. They should actively engage themselves in community efforts to enhance the quality of life. They should, as Morioka suggests, develop to support and assist each other. They should actively create their own "Lotus Villages" rather than relying on prefabricated Potemkin-villages offered by charlatans such as Asahara.

Amazingly, Aum survived its collapse of 1995 and has exhibited considerable growth in the late 1990s. According to the *Asahi Shimbun*[5], by mid 1998 Aum had about 5,500 followers, 15 offices and more than 100 places where followers live together. And the new members were bringing in funds—in the form of membership fees—while sales are growing from at least six Aum-run computer shops in Tokyo. Government officials said that in 1997, sales from these stores exceeded 4 billion yen, while membership fees and admission to the cult's seminars put 24 million yen in the sect's coffers.

Aum has been reaching out to potential followers and former followers through Aum's home page on the Internet. The home page offers information on its history, preachings by Asahara, and messages from its followers. Virtual schools for cult children are also offered through the home page. The home page had been accessed more than 310,000 times by late May, 1998.

These figures suggest that while Asahara's career is certainly over, the questions he and other religious leaders posed to Japanese society are very germane and that the appeal of such organizations will remain unless some concerted effort is made in response.

Appendix I
ಐಿಞ
Cast of Characters in the Aum Shinrikyo Affair

Aoyama Yoshinobu
Aum "Minister of Justice" and chief attorney. Born in March 1960 in Osaka, graduated from Kyoto University Faculty of Law. Worked for Kyodo Law offices before joining Aum in 1988.

Asahara Shoko
Aum Shinrikyo leader. Real name is Matsumoto Chizuo.

Egawa Shoko
Crusading prize-winning journalist whose early articles and books brought attention to Aum as a "dangerous cult" in 1989.

Endo Seiichi
Aum's "Minister of Health and Welfare," chief biologist for Aum and leading figure in Aum's development of chemical and biological weapons. A graduate of Obihiro Veterinary University, he did postgraduate work at the Kyoto University School of Medicine.

Hayakawa Kiyohide
Aum's "Minister of Construction," close advisor to Asahara, and director of Aum's foreign expansion who visited Russia more than 20 times. Press reports indicate that he was second most powerful leader of Aum. Reportedly led Aum's militarization and illegal activities. Born in July 1949 in Osaka and a graduate of Kobe University in agriculture, Worked for various Osaka-based construction companies before joining Aum in 1986.

Hayashi Ikuo
Middle-aged former cardiovascular surgeon and graduate of Keio University Medical School who ran Aum clinics and presided over human experimentation and drugging. Joined Aum in 1990. Sentenced to life imprisonment in 1998.

Inoue Yoshihiro
Aum's "Minister of Intelligence" and leader of Aum's action and hit squads. In charge of gathering information, recruiting, and eliminating dissidents. Only 18 when he joined Aum in 1988.

Hisako Ishii
Aum's "Minister of Finance." Born in September, 1960 and graduate of Industrial Efficiency College. She joined Aum in 1984 and first to experience "emancipation" (*gedatsu*) after Asahara. A devoted follower of Asahara said to be second-in-command during Aum's early years.

Joyu Fumihiro
Aum's "Minister of Foreign Affairs" and chief media spokesman in 1995. A telecommunications graduate of Waseda University in 1984 and, briefly, an employee of Japan's space agency before joining Aum in 1986. Ran Aum's Moscow branch from 1992-95.

Kariya Kiyoshi
Tokyo notary public abducted and killed by Aum in 1995.

Kibe Tetsuya
Chief of Aum's "Defense Agency" and Asahara's personal security.

Lobov, Oleg
Chairman of Russia's Security Council and close aide to President Boris

Yeltsin. Regarded as Aum's most influential supporter in Russia.

Murai Hideo
Aum's "Minister of Science and Technology." Astrophysicist with graduate degree from Osaka University who worked for Kobe Steel in R&D developing special metals for fighter planes before joining Aum in 1989. In charge of Aum's "science" activities and futuristic weapons program research. Murdered on 23 April 1995 in Tokyo.

Nakagawa Tomomasa
Director of Aum's "Household Agency" and Asahara's personal physician. Graduate of Kyoto Prefectural Medical University who quit his internship to join Aum in 1989.

Niimi Tomomitsu
Aum's "Minister of Internal Affairs" and security chief. A central figure in Aum's clandestine activities including surveillance of police activities and kidnapping, retrieval and forced confinement of Aum defectors.

Sakamoto Tsutsumi
Young Yokohama lawyer hired in 1989 by concerned parents of Aum members. Was kidnapped and killed by Aum hit squad in November, 1989 along with his wife and baby son.

Tsuchiya Masami
Aum's chief chemist. Held Ph.D. in organic chemistry from Tsukuba University.

Appendix II
ℰℑℭℜ
Timeline of Events in Aum History[1]

Date	Event
Nov. 1955	Asahara Shoko [real name Matsumoto Chizuo] born in Kumamoto Prefecture.
1977	Asahara moves to Tokyo. Prepares for and then fails Tokyo University entrance exam.
Jan 1978	Asahara marries wife Tomoko. First child born in 1979.
July 1978	Starts "pharmacy" in Chinese herbal medicines. Starts study of various religious practices.
1981	Joins Agonshu—departs in 1984.
1982	Asahara charged, convicted and briefly jailed because of violation of Drug, Cosmetics, and Medical Instruments Act.
Feb 1984	Aum Shinsen no Kai founded by Asahara Shoko.

1985   Asahara begins to claim extraordinary powers and to exhibit an awareness of his qualities as a charismatic leader. In February an occult journal shows picture of Asahara "floating in the air." In November he claims visitation from Hindu God Shiva who "anoints" Asahara the "god of light who leads armies of the gods" to form the ideal society of Shambhala.

1986-87   First of several trips to India / South Asia. On these trips he meets with Hindu and Buddhist religious scholars and leaders and claims to have received enlightenment from them.

July 1987   The name of the organization is changed to Aum Shinrikyo (Aum Supreme Truth Sect). Matsumoto Chizuo changes name to Asahara Shoko for religious purposes.

August 1989   Aum Shinrikyo is recognized as a religious corporation under the terms of the Religious Corporations Law by the Tokyo prefectural government.

Feb. 1989   A dissident Aum member Taguchi Shuji is murdered at Aum headquarters.

Nov. 1989   Sakamoto Tsutsumi, a lawyer representing families of Aum members, disappears with his wife and infant son. An Aum badge is found in the Sakamoto home, but the police fail to find sufficient evidence to warrant any arrests, leaving the case unsolved.

Feb. 1990   Asahara and 24 other Aum members stand for election to the Lower House of the Diet. All twenty-five are very unsuccessful in their attempt [Asahara receives less than 1800 out of a half-million votes cast in his district].

May 1990   Local residents in Namino Village, Kumamoto

Prefecture, oppose Aum's efforts to establish a commune in the village. Charges are brought by both sides, and eventually in August of 1994 the village agrees to pay Aum 920 million yen (over $10 million) in exchange for their agreement to leave the village by August 1997.

Feb 1992
Asahara and entourage travel to Moscow on "Russian Salvation Tour"—the first of three Asahara visits to Russia. Eventually a central office in Moscow and three branch offices are opened. Aum eventually claims an unverified membership of 30,000 Russians.

April 1993
Aum officials buy land for base in Western Australia.

June 1993
A Tokyo resident charges Aum with holding him against his will and demanding his property.

July 1993
Local residents lodge complaints concerning a foul smell emanating from an Aum building under construction in Tokyo.

Sept. 1993
Asahara and Aum team travel to Western Australia; stay for 2-4 weeks.

June 1994
Sarin nerve gas is released in the city of Matsumoto in Nagano Prefecture, killing seven residents. Police investigation centers on a local who first discovered and reported the gas, but no charges are brought. It is also widely reported that a court case concerning Aum was to be decided in Matsumoto, but the case had to be delayed because several of the judges involved were injured by the poison gas.

July 1994
Residents of Kamikuishiki Village in Yamanashi Prefecture near Tokyo, the site of a cluster of Aum facilities, complain of foul odors. Investigations reveal traces of chemicals used in the manufacture of sarin.

Jan 1995   Members of Aum bring charges against several residents of Kamikuishiki for allegedly releasing sarin gas near the Aum facilities. The residents level countercharges against Aum in February.

Feb 1995   Kariya Kiyoshi, the brother of an Aum member, is kidnapped on a Tokyo street. He had opposed his sister's participation in the group, especially her plans to donate sizable family property to Aum. It is later learned that Kariya died in Aum hands. The license of the car used in the crime is traced to an Aum member.

19 March 1995   Three members of Aum are arrested in Osaka for allegedly trying to kidnap a university student who had attempted to leave the religion.

20 March 1995   Poison gas is released in the Tokyo subway system during the morning rush hour, killing 12 and injuring 5500-6000. In the following months there are several more incidents involving noxious gas on the public transportation system in Tokyo and Yokohama.

22 March 1995   Three thousand police raid 25 Aum facilities nationwide. Search warrants are issued in connection with the disappearance the previous month of Kariya Kiyoshi, but the search soon focuses on the stockpiling of chemicals and weapons, and the existence of a chemical plant in the facilities at Kamikuishiki.

23 April 1995   Murai Hideo, chief of Aum's "science and technology program" stabbed to death in Tokyo by man with gangster connections.

16 May 1995   Asahara and 16 other Aum leaders are arrested on suspicion of involvement in subway sarin gas incident.

6 June 1995   Asahara and 6 other Aum leaders indicted on murder and attempted murder charges.

30 Oct 1995	Tokyo District Courts drops recognition of Aum as an authorized religious corporation.
14 Dec 1995	The government decides to pursue the invocation of the Anti-subversive Activities Law to outlaw Aum. First hearing is held in January, 1996.
28 March 1996	Tokyo district court declares Aum bankrupt.
April 1996	Start of Asahara murder trial.
31 Jan 1997	Public Security Commission votes unanimously not to ban Aum under Anti-subversive Activities Law.
19 May 1998	Aum doctor Hayashi Ikuo is sentenced in Tokyo to life imprisonment.

Notes

Preface

1. The name Aum Shinrikyo represents a mixture of Indian and Japanese themes. "Aum" derives from the Sanskrit "Om" and refers to the powers of destruction and creation in the universe.
2. Aum Shinrikyo will be referred to as a religious "sect" throughout this text. Although the popular press has referred to Aum as a "cult," this term is too vague in its meaning and interpretation. Scholars of Japanese religion generally agree with the argument that Aum fits the general definition of a religious "sect."
3. In this work I shall generally refer to the movement as Aum rather than its full name, Aum Shinrikyo, for the sake of brevity.
4. The two best works published by summer 1998 are: Shimazono Susumu, "In the Wake of Aum: The Formation and Transformation of a Universe of Belief" in *Japanese Journal of Religious Studies* 1995 22/3-4, pp. 380-418. Ian Reader, *A Poisonous Cocktail?: Aum Shinrikyo's Path to Violence* (Copenhagen: NIAS Books, 1996).
5. Shimazono, p. 383.
6. Note: This work follows the usual practice of placing all Japanese family names first.

Chapter I

1. Murkami Haruki, "Taking on the Forces of 'Black Magic'" in *The Daily Yomiuri*, 17 May 1998, p. 15.
2. Ian Reader, note to author, 17 September 1997
3. Robert Kisala, "Aum Spiritual Truth Church in Japan" in Anson Shupe, Ed., *Wolves Within the Fold: Religious Leadership and Abuses of Power* (New Brunswick: Rutgers University Press, 1998), pp. 45-46.
4. Many of these religions, including Soka Gakkai actually have prewar roots, but their maturation and greatest growth came after 1945
5. Inagaki Hisakazu, "Religious Cults and Postwar Japanese Society" in *The Japanese Christian Review* (vol. 63, 1997), p. 31;
6. The best study of "The New Age of Japan" is: Haga Manabu and Robert J. Kisala, Eds., "The New Age in Japan" in the *Japanese Journal of Religious Studies*, 22.3-4 (Fall, 1995).
7. Ibid., pp. 31-32.
8. Ibid., p. 33.
9. Ibid.

10. Inagaki Hisakazu, "Religious Cults and Postwar Japanese Society: Aum and Japanese Youth" in *The Japan Christian Review* (63)1997, p. 31.
11. Ibid.

Chapter II

1. *Japan Times*, 17 May 1995, p. 3.
2. There have been various reports in the Japanese media that Asahara has far better eyesight than he and his cohorts have ever claimed.
3. *Asahi Evening News*, 30 September 1995, p. 3.
4. Ishii Kenji, p. 209.
5. Brackett, p. 69.
6. Reader, *A Poisonous Cocktail*, p. 19.
7. Ishii Kenji, p. 210.
8. *Asahi Evening News*, 25 September 1995, p. 3.
9. Ian Reader reports that Asahara anointed his third daughter as his successor and spiritual heir. This is a common practice in Japanese religious terms: "the charisma of leaders is often considered to be passed on through the blood, and it is the normal case that the founder of a religious movement is succeeded by a direct descendent." Reader , *A Poisonous Cocktail,* p. 20.
10 Brackett, p. 70.
11. Ishii Kenji, p. 210.
12. Shimazono writes that although Asahara's acupuncture work went well, he began to feel that his efforts to heal people individually were in vain. A "continuing battle between self-confidence and my complexes" resulted, leaving him "psychologically unstable and assaulted by the uneasy feeling that things could not go on this way....For the first time I stopped and thought, 'What am I living for? What must I do to overcome this sense of emptiness?' This is a feeling which we all experience from time to time, only not as intensely. In a situation like that some people will change jobs, and some people just disappear. However, I set off in a completely different direction. The desire to seek after the infinite, the unchanging, awoke within me, and I began groping for an answer. That meant that I had to discard everything. Yes, everything that I had. It took great courage and faith, and great resolution." Quoted in Shimazono, p. 385.
13. Kisala, p. 2.
14. Takahashi Shinji's teachings, which bore a passing resemblance to Buddhism, emphasized a spiritual world with multiple levels, different realms to which spirits could ascend or descend to at death, and the essential sinful nature of this world.
15. Barret, p. 70.
16. A 1995 Aum Japanese brochure said that there were 1700 renunciates, but most Japanese who have studied Aum place the number at about 1120.

17. Aum as an organization never totally disappeared even after the 16 May 1995 arrest of Asahara. News reports in 1997 and 1998 indicate that the organization is experiencing some new growth under a new leadership. See Epilogue.

18. Richard Young, "Lethal Achievements: Fragments of a Response to the Aum Shinrikyo Affair," in *Japanese Religions* 20.2 (July 1995), pp. 240-241.

19. Aum also bought a sheep ranch in Western Australia in the early mid-1990s where Aum scientists produced and experimented with sarin gas.

20. Aum murdered Sakamoto and his family at their home and buried their bodies in rural western Japan. The June 1994 sarin gas attack in Matsumoto took place in a neighborhood where three of the judges hearing the case lived. Seven innocent people died and many more were injured, including one of the judges, thus forcing a postponement of the case.

21. Interview with Professor Nakano Tsuyoshi at Soka University, May 27, 1996.

22. Shimazono Susumu, "In the Wake of Aum: The Formation and Transformation of a Universe of Belief" in 22:3-4 (Fall 1995), p. 381.

23. Ibid.

Chapter III

1. Quoted in Martin Repp, "Who's the First to Cast the Stone? Aum Shinrikyo, Religions and Society in Japan," in *The Japan Mission Journal*, 49.4 (Winter, 1995), pp. 225-26.

2. Reader, p. 15.

3. Ibid., p. 16.

4. Ibid.

5. Ian Reader, while commenting on an earlier draft of this manuscript, noted this writer's comments on the "inauthenticity" of Aum's stance on and use of various aspects of Buddhism:

    Maybe you overstate the inauthenticity of Aum. After all, it did what pretty much all other new religions [in Japan] did in taking Buddhist sutras and 'interpreting' them in line with its leader's experiences. The same process is seen in Reiyukai, Kofuku, Agonshu, to name but three. While eclectic, Aum certainly used a lot of Buddhist ideas and thoughts....Although some parts of Buddhism do focus on enlightenment (no fixed soul, etc), these points are not universally found in Buddhism. Japanese Buddhist sects in general, despite Buddhist theory, clearly regard the soul as something with a continuing identity—this is the underlying theme of all Buddhist ancestral rites and is found in the publications of Buddhist sects from Soto Zen and Jodo Shin to Shingon. Using Buddhist themes and images is a recurrent element in the new religions—and especially in finding the "original Buddhism" in the very new religions.

6. Ibid., pp. 16-17.

7. His two-volume series *Kirisuto Sengen* (1991-92)—translated as *Declaring Myself the Christ*—contains a picture of Asahara imposed on a cross.

8. Reader, pp. 17-18.

9. Reader, p. 23.
10. Young, p. 236.
11. Ibid., pp. 236-37.
12. Reader, p. 23.
13. Ibid.
14. Asahara provides this explanation of Kundalini:
     Kundalini is a spiritual energy which raises the human spirit to higher dimensions.
     Everyone of us has this energy within us, but it is dormant in an ordinary person. If
     you wish to attain enlightenment, the first thing you must do is to awaken it. This is
     called "the awakening of Kundalini." Buddha Shakyamuni attained enlightenment
     by continuing his practice after he awakened his Kundalini. It was the same with
     me.
     Source: Asahara Shoko, *Beyond Life and Death* (Fujinomiya: Aum Publishing
     Co., 1993), p. 26.
15. Shimazono, p. 388.
16. Shambhala is referred to in some Buddhist texts as an idealized Buddhist
     kingdom based on the highest principles of Buddhist law. According to *the
     Kalacakra Tantra*, an esoteric Buddhist text well known to Asahara, Raudra
     Cakrin, the ideal king of Shambhala, will be reborn as a messiah who defeats
     the infidels in an apocalyptic war and establishes the reign of Buddhism
     throughout the world.
          Asahara imagined that he was that messiah and that he would lead the
     world to this wonderful promised land. Asahara simultaneously stressed that
     he was concerned with more that the salvation of a few individuals, but, rather,
     worldwide salvation.
17. *Asahara Shoko,* Inishieshon [*Initiation*] (Tokyo: Aum Press, 1987).
18. Quoted in Repp, p. 233.
19. Asahara, *Shukyo,* pp. 45-46.
20. Shoko Asahara, *The Teachings of the Truth Vol 3. The Preconditions of the
     True Religion* (Fujinomiya: Aum Publishing Co. Ltd., 1992), pp. 29-30.
21. Asahara Shoko, *Shukyo no jotai* [The Condition of Religion] (Tokyo: Aum
     Press, 1991), p. 90.
22. In an undated, Japanese-language pamphlet distributed to the author on a Kyoto
     street corner in May, 1995, a section devoted to Asahara's spiritual training
     chronicles his meetings with many leading figures of Tibetan Buddhism, including
     Khamtul Rinpoche, Kalu Rinpoche, and the Dalai Lama, who supposedly
     appointed Asahara to be his anointed disciple in Japan. Asahara's meeting with
     the Dalai Lama is described in detail in the following section.
          David Kaplan and Andrew Marshall write that: "The Dalai Lama had a
     slightly different version of events. The Tibetan leader recalled giving Asahara
     no special mission. In fact, he remembered Asahara showing more interest in
     how to structure a religious organization than in Buddhist thought. The Japanese
     was simply one of hundreds of people His Holiness meets each year. According
     to an aide of the Dalai Lama, 'Asahara was nothing special.'" (David Kaplan

and Andrew Marshall, *The Cult at the End of the World: The Incredible Story of Aum* (London: Arrow Books, Ltd., 1996), p. 14.)

The Dalai Lama, in an interview with Japanese reporters on 7 April, 1995 in Tokyo, says that he recalls meeting Asahara in 1987 and on 4-5 subsequent occasions. The Tibetan leader said that he was impressed with Asahara's seriousness and spirituality. "I consider him a friend, but not necessarily a perfect one." Concerning Asahara, The Dalai Lama also noted: "I have met him before, but he was not my disciple or anything." (*Japan Times*, April 8, 1995, p. 3)

A story published in the *Tibetan Review* in early 1991 presents an interesting critique of Aum's claims that it is a truly Buddhist movement with strong ties to the Tibetan tradition:

> For about a year now Tibetans living in Japan have been disturbed by a curious development. Some people are indulging in strange rituals and passing them off as Tibetan Buddhism... It seems the cult now has 2,000 young Japanese followers, and their number is increasing by the day. Their teacher goes under the name of Om Sindhi Khyo, but his real name is known to be Asahara. The rituals he teaches his disciples include practice of yoga, levitation and other acts that are neither Tibetan or Buddhism and are more akin to rituals of Indian sadhus (Hindu ascetics). The teacher as well as the disciples wear flowing white robes, something that no practitioner of Buddhism does.
>
> Tibetans in Japan...are indignant that something that is not Tibetan Buddhism is being taught as Tibetan Buddhism.... Pema Gyalpo of the Tibet Culture Center once went to the [Aum] ashram complaining about their use of the name Tibetan Buddhism. The source says that he was rudely turned back and that some of his students even threatened him with physical assault had he persisted with his efforts. Asahara, the source says, is believed to have told Gyalpo that he has shaken hands with the Dalai Lama and made donations to him. He is reported to have added that the religious department of the Tibetan government approves of his teachings.
>
> Asahara is known to have visited India, including Dharam-sala, at least once. The travel agents handling his trip say he has left a number of hotels in Delhi and Dharamsala without paying his bills.

Source: Republished in *Impact* (30.8), August 1995, p. 31

23. Asahara, *Supreme Initiation, introduction.*
24. Ibid.
25. Shimazono, p. 391.
26. Ibid., p. 392.
27. *Supreme Initiation,* p. 25.
28. Asahara, *Shukyo,* pp. 45-46.
29. Quoted in Brackett, *Holy Terror: Armageddon in Tokyo,* pp. 78-79.
30. Robert Kisala, "Agents of Armageddon." Unpublished manuscript, 1996, p. 4.
31. Repp, p. 239.
32. Ibid.
33. *Teachings of the Truth* Vol. 2, pp. 105-106.
34. *Asahi Shimbun,* 9 September 1995.
35. Barett, p. 88.

36. Kaplan, p. 47.
37. Ibid.
38. Hardacre, p. 14.
39. Shoko Asahara, *Declaring Myself the Christ* (Fujinomiya: Aum Publishing Co., 1992), p. vii. and 71.
40. Ibid., p. 6.
    Concerning the ideal world of Aum before 1990, Asahara wrote:
    If a country has many believers in the teaching of the truth, it won't have any internal conflicts, and will avoid waging a war against foreign countries. As such countries increase, the earth will be more peaceful and secure. So I assert that there will be no battles of any kind...Only Aum can make it possible, because it has an excellent training system. The training system for your emancipation and enlightenment is perfect. If it spreads all over the world, we can avoid World War III. *(Supreme Initiation,* p. 92)
41. Kisala, p. 5.
42. William D. deBary ed., *The Buddhist Tradition in India, China and Japan* (New York: Random House, 1972), p. 112.
43. *Aum Shinrikyo.* Pamphlet (no date) in Japanese distributed to author in May, 1995, pp. 4-6.
44. Shimazono, p. 406.
45. Ibid.
46. Reader, p. 31.
47. Ibid.
48. Shoko Asahara, *Disaster Approaches The Land of the Rising Sun* (Tokyo: Aum Publishing Co., Ltd., 1995), pp. 129-30.
49. Ibid., pp. 14-15.
50. In an earlier version of this manuscript this writer noted that in less than a decade, Aum had moved from meditation to cold-blooded politics. Ian Reader commented that despite this outward appearance of immense change in Aum, the degree of change within the movement itself was not as dramatic. Even in the days around the sarin attack in Tokyo, leading members were sent to meditate and reflect on their deeds. What is interesting is that in the shift to murder, meditation continued to play a large role. Indeed, I suspect Aum could not have sustained its terrorism unless it retained this meditative emphasis (meditation thus serving to confirm the righteousness of murder.@ Letter to author, *op. cit.*
51. Reader, p. 90.
52. According to Shimazono Susumu, "Asahara's knowledge of the concept of Shambala probably comes from the *Kalacakra Tantra,* a later period text valued by esoteric Buddhism. In the *Kalacakra Tantra* transmission, Shambala is imagined to be a hidden valley existing somewhere in northeastern Asia. According to this tradition, in time Raudra Cakrin, the ideal king of Shambala, will be reborn as a messiah to defeat the infidels in a final war and establish the reign of Buddhism. The origin of Asahara's messianic self-awareness can be found here." *Vide,* Shimazono Susumu, "In the Wake of Aum: The Formation

and Transformation of a Universe of Belief" in *Japanese Journal of Religious Studies*, 1995 (22/3-4), pp. 388-89.
53. Reader, p. 31.
54. Robert Kisala, "Agents of Armageddon." Unpublished manuscript (1996), p.4.

Chapter IV

1. Mullins, p. 242.
2. Yukiko Tanaka, *Contemporary Portraits of Japanese Women* (Westport, Connecticut: Praeger, 1995), pp. 74-75.
3. Haruki Murakami, *Norwegian Wood*, v. 1 (Tokyo: Kodansha, 1996), p. 241.
4. Ibid., p. 238.
5. Suzuki Kentaro suggests that palmistry and physiognomy are the most important forms of street fortune telling. Next in popularity are Chinese augury or Eastern astrology. See Suzuki Kentaro, "Divination in Contemporary Japan," in Haga and Kisala, ed., *op. cit.*, pp. 249-266.
6. Haga and Kisala, p. 238.
7. Ibid., pp. 238-39.
8. Ibid., p. 239.
9. Prophecies of Nostradamus, a sixteenth century French astrologer, became best-sellers in Japan when they were translated into Japanese in the 1970s.
10. Haga and Kisala, *op. cit.*, pp. 239-40.
11. "Report: The Religious Situation of the 'Aum Generation,'" in *Japanese Religions*, 22.1 (January, 1997), p. 91.
12. Miyai Rika. "A voice from the 'Aum generation'" in *Japanese Religions* 22/1 (1997): 91-96.
13. Ibid., p. 92.
14. There is no exact translation of the word "Otaku." The closest English equivalent in this context might be "computer nerd."
15. Interview with Watanabe Yuki, 23 June 1997.

Chapter V

1. Nagatomo Sahako, "Yumei Ko Sotsugyosei naze ooii" (why so many graduates from famous schools?), *AERA*, 15 May 1995, PP. 16-17.
2. It is important to note here that although the Aum members polled here were all very well-educated, not all Aum members have such a strong educational background.
3. Ibid.
4. Yamamoto Masamu, "Boku no Aum wa Owaranai," [My Aum will not End] in *AERA*, 5 June 1995, 1995, pp. 6-7.
5. *Asahi Shimbun*, July 9, 1995, p. 4.

6. Noah S. Brannen, "A Religious Response to the Aum Affair," in *Japan Quarterly*, October-December 1995, p. 384.
7. Murakami Haruki , *Andaaguraundo* (underground; Tokyo, 1997).
8. Murakami Haruki, "Taking on the Forces of Black Magic" in *The Daily Yomiuri*, 17 May 1998, p. 15.
9. Frederik L. Schodt, *Dreamland Japan: Writings on Modern Manga* (Berkeley CA: Stone Bridge Press, 1996), p. 230.
10. Ibid.
11. *Aum Comic No. 1,* 30 June 1995.
12. Schodt, p. 232.
13. Ibid., p. 47.
14. Kitabatake Kiyoyasu, "Aum Shinrikyo: Society Begets an Aberration," in *Japan Quarterly*, October-December, 1995, p. 377.
15. *Aum Shinrikyo*, undated pamphlet (distributed to author in Kyoto, May , 1995), pp. 39-47.
16. *Yomiuri Shimbun,* 16 May 1995, p. 3.
17. *Japan Times*, 15 July 1995.
18. Yamaori Tetsuo, "Atheists by Default," *Look Japan*, 41.3 (August 1995), p. 11.
19. Davis, p. 11.
20. *Yomiuri Shimbun,* 27 May 1998, p. 1
21. Irving Hexham and Karla Poewe, *Making the Human Sacred: New Religions as Global Cultures* (Boulder: Westview Press, 1997), p. 9.
22. Watanabe Manabu, "Reactions to the Aum Affair: The Rise of the 'Anti-cult' Movement in Japan" in *Bulletin of the Nanzan Institute for Religion and Culture*, 21, 1997, pp. 32-48.
23. Takahashi Shingo, quoted in Watanabe, p. 41.
24. Watanabe, p. 41.
25. Interview with Watanabe Manabu at Nanzan University, 5 June 1997
26. Aum's first victim, a young recruit named Taguchi, was murdered not because he was a potential defector, but, rather, because he had evidence that another Aum member had died in an Aum ascetic rite that went wrong. Asahara probably felt that both he and Aum would lose credibility if Taguchi leaked news of the death to the press. Asahara possibly ordered Taguchi's execution because he felt that Aum's mission was greater than an individual life and that he had to preserve the mission at all costs.
27. Richard Young, "Lethal Achievements: Fragments of a Response to the Aum Shinrikyo Affair" in *Japanese Religions*, 20.2 (1995), p. 234.
28. Ibid., p. 235.
29. Ibid., p. 238. Young adds that had he paid much closer attention to Aum as a scholar, he would have found that Aum in fact was selling all kinds of "magicoreligious products" for hefty fees.
30. Ibid., pp. 239-40.

Chapter VI

1. Murakami Haruki, "Posuto-Andaaguraundo-#3" (Post-Underground #3 in *Bungei Shunju* 98.6, pp 262-75.)
2. Martin Repp, "Youth and New-New Religions: Challenges for the Churches in Present-Day Japan" in *The Japan Christian Review*, 6.3 (1997), pp. 20-22.
3. Quoted in Judith Miller, "Japanese Cult That Used Nerve Gas Has Resurfaced," *New York Times, 11* October 1998. Miller notes that almost 200 of some 1400 monks investigated by security officers in 1995 were university students or graduates.
4. Young, *op. Cit.,* pp. 233-40.
5. Asako Takaesu, "The Logic of Altered States" in *The Japan Times Weekly,* 29 April 195, pp. 8-9.
6. Takahashi Hidetoshi, *Aum Kara no Kikan* [Coming Back from Aum]. Tokyo: Soshisha, 1996.
7. *Japan Times,* 1 June 1995.
8. Quoted from Repp, pp. 20-22.
9. Derived from "Aum My God! The True Story of an American Married to a Member of the Aum Shinrikyo Cult" in *The Alien*, May 1997, pp. 6-8.

Chapter VII

1. Oki Kazuharo, "Doko e iku shinja sanmannin?" [What will become of the 30,000 believers," in *AERA*, 25 May 1995, p. 35.
    The source of this figure is the chief Russian security office, the former KGB.
2. The main source for this section is the English-language Aum publication, *Monthly Truth*, No. 11, January 1994. Hereafter abbreviated as MT94.
3. See Kaplan, 190-98.
4. MT94, p. 2.
5. Oki, p. 35.
6. Ibid., p. 5.
7. Ibid., p. 15
8. Ibid., pp. 4-5.
9. Oki, pp. 35-36.
10. MT94, p. 26.
11. *AERA* places the core membership at 300 based on reports from Russian intelligence sources. See Oki op. cit., p. 36.
12. Just as in Japan, some Russian families with Aum members joined together and petitioned a Russian court to give them access to their relatives living in Aum communities. The Court ordered all Japanese Aum members to return to Japan and the Aum organization in Russia to be disbanded in March 1995.
13. Kaplan, 195-98.

14. Kaplan, p. 70.
15. Ogi Kazuharu reports in *AERA* that Asahara's offer of large donations for the Japan-Russia university project that brought Aum to the attention of Russian leaders and facilitated Asahara's first visit four months later. See Ogi, p. 36.
16. Oki, pp. 35-37 and Kaplan, 190-95.
17. *Asahi Shimbun*, 31 October 1995.
18. According to David Kaplan and Andrew Marshall:
    One follower, named "David," sounded strikingly like his counterparts in Japan, when interviewed in 1995 by Nippon Television. Asked about the end of the world, the nineteen-year-old religious studies major at Columbia University had this to say: "I believe in Armageddon, in the sense that there will be a catastrophic war between the United States and Japan, that the U.S. will attack Japan, and the world will go into chaos." The coming apocalypse, he added, was "purification of the karma."
    How did he feel about Shoko Asahara? the reporter asked.
    "He's the person I respect most."
    "Which part of him?"
    "His desire to end the suffering of all beings in the universe, to sacrifice his own happiness, his own peace of mind, and give peace to other individuals."
    Source: Kaplan and Marshall, p. 101.
19. Kaplan, p. 101.
20. Derived from Commander Jeff Penrose, "Western Australian link to Japanese Doomsday Cult" in *Platypus Magazine*, December 1995, pp. 5-10, and Kaplan, pp. 126-134..
21. Kaplan, p. 133.
22. Ibid., p. 103.

Chapter VIII

1. See Paul Ginnetty, "Breaking down Heaven's Gate" in *The Japan Times*, 6 April 1997 for a poignant analysis of the members of the Heaven's Gate cult.
2. Kisala, *Aum Spiritual Truth*, p. 46.
3. *Shukyo naki jidai o ikirutame ni* (To Live in an Age of No Religions). Tokyo: Hozokan, 1996.
4. Quoted in Inagaki, p. 35.
5. *Asahi Shimbun*, 26 May 1998, p. 1.

Appendix II

1. Derived in part from Robert Kisala, "Aum Alone in Japan: Religious Responses to the 'Aum Affair'" in *Bulletin of the Nanzan Institute for Religion & Culture*, 19 (1995), pp. 6-8, Inoue Nobutaka et al., *Aum Shinrikyo to wa nanika* (Tokyo: Asahi News Shop, 1995), and *Asahi Shimbun*, 1 February 1997.

Bibliography

Aera Henshubu. *Aum Maho o Toku. AERA* No. 23 (25 May 1995). Tokyo: Asahi Shimbunsha, 1995.

Arita Yoshifu, "Armageddon" in *AERA,* 25 May 1995, pp. 11-13.

Asahi Evening News, "The Man They Call Guru." Six-part series. 25 Oct.-1 Nov 1995.

Asahi Shimbun. 15 May 1995; 9 July 1995; 30 July 1995; 8 August 1995; 17 August 1995; 5-10 and 21-25 September 1995; 5-14, 28 October 1995, 1 November 1995; 17 May 1998.

"Aum My God!: The true story of an American married to a member of the Aum Shinrikyo Cult" in *The Alien,* May 1997, pp. 6-8.

———, *"Aum to Watashi: 50jin ni iku,"* [Aum and I: 50 personal inquiries], *AERA,* 25 May 1995, pp. 19-35.

Brackett, Noah S. *Holy Terror: Armageddon in Tokyo.* New York: Weatherhill, 1996.

Brannen, Noah S. "A Religious Response to the Aum Affair" in the *Japan Quarterly,* October-December 1995, pp. 384-390.

Caldwell, Thomas. "An Encounter with Murai" in the *Japan Times Weekly* (35.17) 29 April 1995, p. 16.

Clarke, Peter B. and Jeffry Somers, eds., *Japanese New Religions in the West* (Sandgate, Folkestone, Kent UK: Japan Library 1994.

Davis, Winston. "Dealing with Criminal Religions: The Case of Om Supreme Truth" in *Christian Century* 19-26 July 1995, p. 10.

De Bary, William D., ed. *The Buddhist Tradition in India, China and Japan.* New York: Random House, 1972.

Egawa Shoko. *Kyuseishu no Yabo.* Tokyo: Kyoikushiryo Shuppankai, 1995.

Fukunaga Hiroshi. "Aum Sweet Home" in *Tokyo Business (*June 1995), pp. 8-12.

Garon, Sheldon. *Molding Japanese Minds: The State in Everyday Life.* Princeton: Princeton University Press, 1997.

Haga Manabu and Robert J. Kisala. "The New Age in Japan: Editors' Introduction" in *Japanese Journal of Religious Studies* (22:3-4) Fall 1995, pp. 235-48.

Hardacre, Helen. "Aum Shinrikyo and the Japanese Media: The Pied Piper Meets the Lamb of God." Institute Reports of the East Asian Institute, Columbia

University, 1996.

Head, Anthony. "Aum's Incredible Journey Toward Armageddon" in the *Japan Quarterly,* October-December 1996, pp. 92-95.

Hexhgam, I. And K. Poewe. *New Religions as Global Cultures.* Boulder: Westview, 1997.

Hirsh, M. "Lost Souls" in *Newsweek* (Asian Edition), 29 May 1995, p. 10.

Ihara Keiko. *"Shukyo ga kimochi yokatta"* ["The Religious Practice was Good"], *AERA* 25 May 1995, pp. 14-15.

Inagaki Hisakazu, "Religious Cults and Postwar Japanese Society: Aum and Japanese Youth" in *The Japan Christian Review* (63) 1997, pp. 30-36.

Inoue Nobutaka, Takeda Michio and Kitabatake Kiyoyasu. *Aum Shinrikyo tɔ wa nanika* [What is Aum Shinrikyo?]. Tokyo: Asahi News Shop, 1995.

Ishii Kenji. "Aum Shinrikyo" in Tamaru Noriyoshi and David Reid, eds., *Religion in Japanese Culture: Where Living Traditions Meet a Changing World.* Tokyo: Kodansha International, 1996.

Iwao Sumiko, "Commentary on Aum" in *Japan Echo,* 22.3 (Fall, 1995).

Japan Times. 8 April and 1 June, 1995

Japan Times Weekly. 29 April, 24 July, 21 August, 1995.

Kajimoto Takeshi. "Mind-Set: Some Cults Cash in on Craving to Belong" in *Japan Times Weekly*, 29 May 1995.

Kaplan, David E. and Andrew Marshall. *The Cult at the End of the World: The Incredible Story of Aum.* London: Arrow Books Ltd, 1996.

Kisala, Robert. "Living in a Post-Aum World" in the *Bulletin of the Nanzan Institute for Religion and Culture,* No. 20 (1996), pp. 7-18

———. "Reactions to Aum: The Revision of the Religious Corporations Law" in *Japanese Religions* (22-1), January 1997, pp. 60-74.

———. "Agents of Armageddon." Unpublished ms.

———. "The AUM Spiritual Church in Japan" in Anson Shupe, ed., *Wolves With the Fold: Religious Leadership and Abuses of Power*, pp. 33-48. New Brunswick, NJ: Rutgers University Press, 1998.

Kitabatake Kiyoyasu. "Aum Shinrikyo: Society Begets an Aberration" in *Japan Quarterly*, October-December 1995, pp. 376-383.

Kitagawa, Joseph. *Religion in Japanese History.* New York: Columbia University Press, 1966.

Lawrence, Richard. *Unlock Your Psychic Powers.* New York: St. Martin's Press, 1993.

LoBreglio, John. "Revisions to the Religious Corporations Law: An Introduction and Annotated Translation" in *Japanese Religions* (22-1), January 1997, pp. 38-59.

Maeda Daisuke. "The Revenge of the Children" in *Japanese Religions* (22.1) 1997, pp. 87-91.

Metraux, Daniel. "Religious Terrorism in Japan: The Fatal Appeal of Aum Shinrikyo" in *Asian Survey* (XXXV.12) December 1995, pp. 1140-54.

———. "Aum Shinrikyo and Japanese Youth" in *Japanese Studies Review* (1998) Vol. 2, pp. 69-81.

———. "Aum Sweet Home: The Appeal of Aum Shinrikyo to Japan's Restless and Depressed Youth" in *American Asian Review* (XV.3), Fall 1997, pp. 191-210.

———. *The Soka Gakkai Revolution.* Lanthan MD: University Press of America, 1994.

Miyai Rika, "A Voice from the 'Aum Generation'" in *Japanese Religions* (22.1) 1997 pp. 91-96.

Morioka Masahiro. *Shukyo naki jidai o ikirutame ni* (To Live in an age of no religions). Tokyo: Hozokan, 1996.

Mullins, Mark R. , Shimazono Susumu and Paul L. Swanson. eds, *Religion and Society in Modern Japan.* Berkeley: Asian Humanities Press, 1993.

Mullins, Mark. "Japan's New Age and Neo-New Religions" in James R. Lewis and J. Gordon Melton, *Perspectives on the New Age.* Albany: SUNY 1992.

———. "The Political and Legal Response to Aum-Related Violence in Japan" in *The Japan Christian Review* (63) 1997, pp. 37-46.

Murakami Haruki. *Norwegian Wood.* Tokyo: Kodansha 1996.

———. *Andaaguraundo* (Underground). Tokyo: Hozokan, 1997.

———. *"Posuto-andaaguraundo*(Post-Underground) *(3) "* in *Bungei Shunju* June 1998. pp. 262-275.

———. "Taking on the forces of 'Black Magic'" in *The Daily Yomiuri,* 17 May 1998.

Nagatomo Sahako, *"Yumei kokosotsugyosei ooi"* [The number of graduates from famous high schools was great] in *AERA,* 15 May 1995.

Nakano Tsuyoshi. "New Religions and Politics in Postwar Japan," in *Sociologica (14. 12)* 1990, pp. 3-12.

New York Times. 22 May 1995 and 11 October 1998.

Nihon Shimbun Kyokai. *The Japanese Press 1996.* Tokyo: NSK, 1996.

Nomura Yoshihiko. "Where Aum is Coming From" in *Kansai Forum,* June-July 1995, pp. 15-18.

Norbeck, Edward. *Religion and Society in Modern Japan.* Houston: Tourmaline, 1970.

O'Brien, David M. *To Dream of Dreams: Religious Freedom and Constitutional Politics in Postwar Japan.* Honolulu: U Hawaii Press, 1996.

Oki Kazuharu, *"Roshia: doko e iku shinja nimannin"* [Where Will 20,000 Believers in Russia Go?] in *AERA,* 25 May 1995, pp. 35-37.

Penrose, J. "Western Australian Link to Japanese Doomsday Cult" in *Platypus Magazine,* December 1995, pp. 5-10.

Pye, Michael. "Aum Shinrikyo: Can Religious Studies Cope?" in *Religion,* (26) 1996, pp. 261-270.

Reader, Ian. *A Poisonous Cocktail? Aum Shinrikyo's Path to Violence.* Copenhagen: NIAS Publications, 1996.

———. "The Rise of a Japanese 'New New Religion': Themes in the Development of Agonshu" in *Japanese Journal of Religious Studies*, (15.1) 1988, pp. 235-61.

———. *Religion in Contemporary Japan.* Honolulu: U Hawaii Press, 1991.

———. "The Religious Situation of the 'Aum Generation': Two NCC Seminars" in *Japanese Religions (22-1)* January 1997, pp. 87-98.

Repp, Martin. "Who's the First to Cast the Stone? Aum Shinrikyo, Religions and Society in Japan" in *The Japan Mission Journal* (49.4) Winter 1995, p. 225-255.

———. "Youth and New-New Religions: Challenges for the Churches in Present-Day Japan" in *The Japan Christian Review* (63) 1997, pp. 5-29.

Sato Michio. "Burying the Truth of an Assassination Attempt" in the *Asahi Evening News,* 11 July 1997.

Shimatsu Yoichi. "Here and Now" in the *Japan Times Weekly* (35.17) 29 April 1995.

Shimazono Susumu. "In the Wake of Aum: The Formation and Transformation of a Universe of Belief" in *Japanese Journal of Religious Studies* (22.3-4) Fall 1995, pp. 381-416.

Shimizu Masato, ed. *Shinshukyo jidai* [the era of new religions]. Tokyo: Okura Shuppan, 1995.

Schodt, Frederik L. *Dreamland Japan: Writings on Modern Manga* Berkeley CA: Stone Bridge Press, 1996.

Takasu Asako. "The Piano of the Mind" and "The Logic of Altered States" in the *Japan Times Weekly* (35.17) 29 April 1995, pp. 10-11.

Takahashi Hidetoshi. *Aum Kara no Kikan* (Coming Back from Aum). Tokyo: Soshisha, 1996.

Tanaka Yukiko. *Contemporary Portraits of Japanese Women.* Wesport CT: Praeger, 1995.

Tetsu Yamaori. "Athiests by Default" in *Look Japan*, August 1995, pp. 11-12.

Watanabe Manabu, "Reactions to the Aum Affair: The Rise of the 'Anti-Cult' Movement in Japan" in the *Bulletin of the Nanzan Institute for Culture And Religion,* 21 (1997), pp. 32-48.

Yamamoto Masao. *"Boku no Aum wa owaranai" [My life with Aum will not end], AERA* , 5 June 1995, pp. 6-7.

———. *"Kagakusha Gruupu no hontoo no jitsuryoku"* [The True Power of the Scientist Group], *AERA*, 15 May 1995, pp. 8-9.

Yomiuri Shimbun. 16 May and 17 September 1995.

Young, Richard."Lethal Achievements: Fragments of a Response to the Aum Shinrikyo Affair in *Japanese Religions* (20.2) 1995, pp. 230-45.

Aum Shinrikyo Publications:

Aum Comics. June 1995.
Aum Shinrikyo. Undated pamphlet in Japanese received by author May 1995.
"The Great Guru Asahara," Nos. 1+2, 1991.
Mahayana News Letter: Vol. 13 (September 1989); Vol. 14 (October, 1989); Vol. 15 (December 1989); Vol. 24 (August 1991); Vol. 25 (October 1991).
Monthly Truth: Liberation from Suffering and Enlightenment: No. 14 (January 1994); No. 20 (January/February 1995); No. 21 (Summer 1995).

Aum Shinrikyo Publications by Asahara Shoko:

Beyond Life and Death. Fujinomiya: Aum Publishing Co. Ltd, 1993.
Declaring Myself the Christ: Disclosing the True Meanings of Jesus Christ's Gospel. Fujinomiya: Aum Pub., 1992.
Disaster Approaches the Land of the Rising Sun. Tokyo: Aum , 1995.
Shukyo no jotai [The Condition of Religion]. Tokyo: Aum, 1991.
Supreme Initiation: An Empirical Spiritual Science for the Supreme Truth. New York: Aum USA, 1992.
The Teachings of the Truth, vols. 1-5. Fujinomiya: Aum, 1991-93.

Index